Also by Ann Beattie

Mrs. Nixon

A Novelist Imagines a Life

Ann Beattie

Scribner

New York   London   Toronto   Sydney   New Delhi

Scribner
A Division of Simon & Schuster, Inc.
1230 Avenue of the Americas
New York, NY 10020

Copyright © 2011 by Ann Beattie

All rights reserved, including the right to reproduce this book or portions
thereof in any form whatsoever. For information address Scribner Subsidiary Rights
Department, 1230 Avenue of the Americas, New York, NY 10020.

First Scribner hardcover edition November 2011

SCRIBNER and design are registered trademarks of The Gale Group, Inc., used under
license by Simon & Schuster, Inc., the publisher of this work.

For information about special discounts for bulk purchases,
please contact Simon & Schuster Special Sales at 1-866-506-1949
or business@simonandschuster.com.

The Simon & Schuster Speakers Bureau can bring authors to your live event.
For more information or to book an event contact the Simon & Schuster Speakers
Bureau at 1-866-248-3049 or visit our website at www.simonspeakers.com.

Designed by Carla Jayne Jones

Manufactured in the United States of America

3   5   7   9   10   8   6   4   2

Library of Congress Cataloging-in-Publication Data is available.

ISBN 978-1-4391-6871-4
ISBN 978-1-4391-6873-8 (ebook)

A portion of the poem "Skinny-Dipping with Pat Nixon" by David Kirby appears
courtesy of the poet. The article "Patricia Nixon, Wife of Former President, Dies at 81"
is reprinted with permission of the *Los Angeles Times* (Copyright © 1993 *Los Angeles
Times*). The logo for *The Tech* is reprinted with permission of *The Tech*.

For Jane and Bob Hill

A note on the book: What you will read is based on research. There is a chronology appended that will allow the reader to know when certain events or moments in Mrs. Nixon's life occurred. Also at the back of the book there are notes that correspond to individual sections. I imagine dialogue to which I had no access; I do my best to write as I think my characters would think and speak, based on what I've read about them. In some cases, factual events are used only as points of departure, which should become clear; those times I write fiction will be recognizable as such. The majority of events, letters, and names are real. (As a young man, Richard Nixon did date Ola Florence Welch; King Timahoe was the Nixons' dog; Henry Kissinger was Secretary of State.) My readings of many texts, from a story by Maupassant to the play *The Romantic Age,* are conveyed as I understand them.

Tuck is given credit (he denies it, somewhat hollowly) for putting on an engineer's hat and waving the Nixon train along in 1960, somewhat enraging the candidate who had just begun a rear platform speech. He is also alleged to have rapped sharply on the glass of the driver's compartment in the Nixon campaign bus one day in Iowa, ordering the driver to start up. He did. The only problem was that Mrs. Nixon was still in town, a fact that was not discovered until the caravan was several miles down the road.

—Frank Mankiewicz, *Perfectly Clear: Nixon from Whittier to Watergate*

Mrs. Nixon

Mrs. Nixon's Nicknames, Including Her Code Name as First Lady

Buddy
Miss Vagabond
Irish Gypsy
St. Patrick's Babe in the Morn
Babe
Pat
Miss Pat
Patricia
Dearest Heart
The White Sister
Starlight

The Lady in the Green Dress

In *The Selling of the President 1968*, Joe McGinniss has described a TV broadcast during which Mr. Nixon faced some hard questions about his stance on Vietnam. After the show ended, "Roger Ailes went looking for Nixon. He wound up in an elevator with Nixon's wife. She was wearing a green dress and she did not smile. One thought of the remark a member of Nixon's staff had made: 'Next to her, RN looks like Mary Poppins.'

"'Hello, Mrs. Nixon,' Roger Ailes said.

"She nodded. She had known him for months.

"'How did you like the show?' he asked.

"She nodded very slowly; her mouth was drawn in a thin, straight line.

"'Everyone seems to think it was by far the best,' Ailes said. 'Especially the way he took care of that McKinney.'

"Pat Nixon stared at the elevator door. The car stopped. The door opened. She got off and moved down a hallway with the Secret Service men around her."

Her possible thoughts?

Mr. Ailes is a loyal supporter, but these people can be a bit naïve.

Or: It pleases Mr. Ailes very much to think he's found the way to elicit a positive response from me. Why should I comply just to please him?

Perhaps: "Mr. Ailes, has it ever occurred to you that I'm a serious person, and that the conclusions you have drawn with such certainty are expedient and self-serving?"

"If I were a vain woman I might turn the subject to myself—the same way, by being so outspoken, you turn the subject as much to yourself as to my husband. And so I might ask you whether you didn't think this was the dandiest dress you'd seen in a long time, and whether we shouldn't applaud: for my husband; for the advent of television; for your job; for my dress, which I tailored myself. What do you say, Dr. Pangloss?"

"Mr. Ailes, do you find it possible to think that yes, I am Mrs. Nixon, but I am also a woman on her way somewhere, that I am just passing through in a perfunctory way, and that even if I were to answer, whatever I say does not really matter?"

Better: "Will you remember tomorrow, Mr. Ailes, that when we spoke I was wearing a green dress? I will certainly remember that you were wearing a white shirt, because you don't have as much leeway as I do, or the freedom most any woman does, about how to dress."

"Forgive me for not answering, but the truth is that I am thinking about my own neatly styled hair and clothing. I don't have to say a word, but you more or less have to say something to me, don't you? So why not admire the dress I bought at Lord & Taylor and paid too much for, instead of pretending my husband is the only topic of interest. If you liked it, I might think better of you."

"Oh, excuse me, I would so love to stay and discuss this, but you see, I brought my pet tortoise with me and it has run away, and I must try to find it before it buries itself in the dirt that is our lives."

"Mr. Ailes, I may very well have forgotten to turn off the bathwater."

Stories as Preemptive Strikes

Mrs. Nixon (before she was Mrs. Nixon) had many nicknames, and one of them was Buddy. She liked the nickname because she felt her given name did not suit her. It's hard to imagine that anyone would be thrilled to be named Thelma. Her mother insisted on naming her that for reasons unknown. The baby's father—who maintained she had been born later than the time of her actual birth—called her his St. Patrick's Babe in the Morn (soon shortened simply to Babe). As far as I can tell, she was born somewhere near midnight the day preceding St. Patrick's Day, 1912, though that doesn't really detract from her father's fondly effusive Irish feeling. Babe lasted for quite a while as a nickname, though Buddy intruded in childhood. Buddy suggests a tomboy, and perhaps any girl who grew up on a farm and did chores and took the dusty world as her playground would seem tomboyish, but as with so much about Mrs. Nixon, new and reliable information recedes with time. Upon entering college, Thelma became, at her own behest, Patricia, then was referred to as Pat, carrying her about as far away from someone else's intention about her identity as most people dared go in those days.

A lot of fiction writers I know own a book called *What Shall We Name the Baby?* because in the heat of writing—or even after cold deliberation—even the simplest name just won't pop into the writer's head. The name Ann is forgotten, Jim unremembered. Sometimes writers want to consider etymology, or to use New Age names to express the mystical quality of the child, or some quality that is hoped for—but I'm thinking of something else: the writer's panicky sense that all names have escaped him or her, and unless the writer can immediately find something ("Jane!"), the character will evaporate before ever being realized. Writers will tell you that when they remembered the name John, suddenly everything became possible. But because they have to look up a name, when no name can be conjured up, they have this book near their desks—unless the writers write on the kitchen counter, say, and then they have it in the fruit bowl. (Think about how many prospective grandmothers have been misled by noticing this book.)

Buddy. Names, nicknames, they're fascinating to writers, but they also cause anxiety because they're so elusive, and because writers have to come up with so many of them. Few people have a gift for the perfect name or nickname, and many such adult monikers are given without the victims' awareness. Henry Kissinger, for example, called Haldeman and Ehrlichman "the Fanatics." (H. R. Haldeman was Nixon's Chief of Staff; John Ehrlichman, Assistant to the President for Domestic Affairs.) Children have to accept their names, at least until they can protest. I don't know how Mrs. Nixon felt about being Buddy. Bottom line, most of us only really want nicknames invented by those we love. My husband has so many nicknames for me that it's lucky we don't have pets. When he calls, I answer to most anything: that day's nickname will undoubtedly be something I don't recognize except for the tone. The only time I stop dead is when he calls me Ann. When he addresses me directly, I'm in trouble. Thelma/Buddy/Pat may have answered to even more names, but we'll never know.

I think of her, though, as Mrs. Nixon. Perhaps Richard Nixon thought of her as Pat or as some endearment we don't know, such as Fuzzy Bunny, but when he referred to her, it was usually as Mrs. Nixon. An egoist like Nixon would of course see people as extensions of himself, so that when he was referring to his wife he was implying a certain dignity, insisting upon the respect he felt was inherent in the position she occupied (thanks to him). Since he often spoke of himself as "he," which is much more bizarre, it's understandable that he would refer to his wife formally. He thought aloud and liked to fabricate stories, and if he hadn't been president, many of his fictions would be highly hilarious, but you're stopped from laughing about this dissociation when you realize that he had control of the "red telephone"—its nickname is the only way it's referred to—and that when he was drunkenly wandering the corridors of the White House talking to the portraits hung on the walls (according to Edward, a.k.a. Eddie, Cox, his son-in-law), one of them might have answered and told him to go make mischief by holding down the little button.

In thinking aloud, he often used the expression "and so forth" as a kind of shorthand for what didn't need to be elaborated—especially since he was often talking to himself. He was his own best audience, and his predictable gestures, his distinctive mannerisms, must have felt like reassuring forms of applause, replacing the usual hand clapping. Nixon—like many politicians—while often in the presence of other people, was essentially talking to himself. He devised stories for others to tell, whether or not they were the truth, then played devil's advocate, becoming first the lawyer for the prosecution, then for the defense, because he *was* a lawyer, and that is the way lawyers think. He did this out of the courtroom, however, and got to keep the witnesses as long as he wanted, or to dismiss them instantly, whichever seemed more advantageous. He was accustomed to hearing his own voice; others lay buried in the landslide of words. He is reported to have made fifty-one phone calls in one night during the Watergate mess—though that was certainly a worse quagmire than most of us ever experience.

Nixon and his team are described by longtime *New Yorker* writer Jonathan Schell in *The Time of Illusion* this way: "The Nixon Administration was characterized by, among other things, fragmentation. What the Nixon men thought was unconnected to what they said. What they said was unconnected to what they did. What they did or said they were doing at one moment was unconnected to what they did or said they were doing the next moment. And when they were driven from office, they left behind them not one but several unconnected records of themselves."

In their feints and dodges, Nixon and his players exhibited a versatility that equaled the range of professional actors. A later leader, Ronald Reagan, would be wittily described by Gore Vidal as "the acting President," but Nixon may have outdone him in the projection of personal fantasy. Often, Nixon elaborated scenarios he knew would never materialize, tacitly encouraging the listeners' imagination, then revealing his own opinion. The outlandish CIA operative and pseudonymous mystery writer E. Howard Hunt put on a red wig to go off on assignment—or what he understood to be an assignment, or imagined to be one because he considered his thinking superior to that of those who might give him an assignment—while also understanding that playing the crazy could not really hurt him. Truly crazy people would buy into his game, and the people who weren't could always dismiss him if things backfired. When not helpful, Hunt was a wild card that could be discarded in the fast and loose nonrules of the game: he was—you know—*not quite right.*

As covert operatives, E. Howard Hunt and G. Gordon Liddy, the caterpillar-mustached leader of the White House "plumbers," were like Rosencrantz and Guildenstern run amok. Jonathan Schell writes that Liddy thought it would be a good plan to hire expensive prostitutes to "lure Democrats to a yacht rigged with secret cameras and recording equipment. The cost would be about a million dollars. [Attorney General John] Mitchell found the plan too expensive, and rejected it." The government was presided over by a president who was most at ease when he could consider many possibilities and all their variables; what might sound comical and sophomorically contrived to most people would always seem to him truly unique, viable options. John Belushi, had he come along a bit earlier, could have led the way—as almost any of his characters but perhaps most helpfully as Samurai Chef.

But we have come far from Mrs. Nixon; such drift seems endemic to writing about the quietly loyal and enigmatic Mrs. Nixon. It is difficult not to leave her behind, when the madness that surrounded her eclipsed her so thoroughly. She knew that Haldeman did not like her, and she did not like Haldeman. He was not even respectful of formalities. He excluded her. Travel schedules were drawn up that simply did not include her. Nothing suggests that she was happy about her husband remaining in politics, but rather that the opposite was true. However, she was used to taking care of things, herself included. Her mother died when she was thirteen, and her father died soon afterward. Mrs. Nixon's daughter Julie recounts a story in which Mrs. Nixon, leaving her mother's funeral, "walked directly over to her friends and said quickly, 'Didn't she look beautiful?'" Mrs. Nixon was telling her friends a story, not asking a question. She was making a preemptive strike, taking command (or appearing to take command) of the situation and offering a remark that, while uninspired and conventional, also asked a hidden question: Won't you believe me?—because I am at risk if you don't. When people believe, Tinker Bell gets to spread her magic.

There's something awkward or even painful for the recipient of such platitudes: the content is of course unremarkable—that is precisely the person's intention—but the storyteller is silently asking for collusion, for an acceptance of this story as it's recited, as opposed to the real story, so that the real story doesn't have to be told, or emotionally registered. In stories, there are two components: what the story is, and how or why it is told. Those things often create the friction in what we're reading. It is usually only through time, or with dropped hints, however, that we can tell someone is an unreliable narrator. Unreliable narrators, of course, do not necessarily know they're unreliable. They can be genuinely ill-informed or simply mistaken, as well as being schemers. When we're reading a work of fiction, the question becomes: does the writer believe this narrator? Lesson one in book club is probably not to assume the voice in the book reflects the outlook of the author. Even quite sophisticated readers can be thrown off by who they think the writer is, though—always a liability for an author, as well as something the writer can capitalize on; paradoxically, once an author is known, there's a temptation to conflate his or her personality with the character's. I once thought about *Felicia's Journey*: William Trevor must be writing about someone who is a nice old man, and who therefore can't have the ominous undercurrents I've started to sense, so it has to be my paranoia. The gentleman, like Trevor himself, would no doubt be a benign creature. It's a good trick, to throw off readers because of who they—the writers—seem to be, but it's not a trick writers can pull too often. I didn't anticipate what was coming in *Felicia's Journey* because of my unconscious stereotyping of the author, and what his fictional world was likely to be. Are we familiar enough with Mrs. Nixon to think that in framing her mother's death as she did she hoodwinked her audience, or herself? Does any author speculating on Mrs. Nixon need to decide whether she creates her one-sentence story with great craft or naïve simplicity?

The Nixon administration helped create a culture of distrust that flourishes today. Inherent faith in government morphed into automatic distrust of all "they" do. We may have become suspicious of narrators because we're so attuned to the discrepancy between the presumptive story and what underlies it. If things are moving and taking shape covertly, the words of the story, read too literally, may come to be an impediment to understanding. To some extent, a reading depends on how secure and knowledgeable the reader is. Sometimes when I'm teaching I read a paragraph aloud to make the point that an interesting tone is present if readers allow themselves to hear it. "But how do you know to read it that way? Of course if you read it like that it's ominous/funny/significant," a student will usually respond. I can always be wrong, but I've come up with my possible reading because the writer has cued me. There has been a subtle alteration before or after the line I've read aloud, or sometimes both. It's bracketed, in effect. A rhythm has been varied, thereby setting something apart while seeming to include it merely as an integer in the story's larger context. In the context of her mother's death, what tone can we deduce from Mrs. Nixon's "Didn't she look beautiful?"

Raymond Carver is amazingly good at altering tone and pacing, using repetition of what's obvious in the action almost as an anesthetic swab that precedes the shot. In "Are These Actual Miles?" Carver works with staccato sentences to hypnotize the reader. He narrates a story about a married couple who are complicitous in what they're doing: the wife is not merely selling their car on the eve of their declaring bankruptcy, she's also selling herself sexually to the used car salesman. Her husband, Leo, waiting at home for news he hopes to hear and news he does not want to hear (they are synonymous), is described: "His undershirt is wet: he can feel the sweat rolling from his underarms. He sits on the step with the empty glass in his hand and watches the shadows fill up the yard. He stretches, wipes his face. He listens to the traffic on the highway and considers whether he should go to the basement, stand on the utility sink, and hang himself with his belt. He understands he is willing to be dead."

If the undershirt is wet, then it follows that he is sweating, so we accept the sweat rolling. If he sits on a step with an empty glass instead of a full glass, he's watching the shadows in a different way than he would if he had a drink, so, okay, they "fill up the yard" (shadows are doing what the liquor is not doing—there's none in the glass). He makes two conventional gestures: stretching and wiping his face. Then we move a bit outside him—he moves a bit outside himself—and he's reminded/we are reminded that there is a larger world, a world of "traffic on the highway." We've moved from something small and personal, how he feels in his damp shirt, to not knowing how he feels exactly (he doesn't tell us here), but we register the other people driving cars (a loaded subject in this story, given what his wife has set out to do) on the big highway, with their inherently metaphorical connotations.

This is already a lot to keep track of, though nothing much is happening overtly: we've moved from the personal to the larger world, but a world that is nevertheless eluding the character. We go from close-up to long shot. *We* are considering him from a lot of angles, so it may even come as a slight relief to know that he's doing some considering, too. Except that in completing this sentence—as opposed to the ones that have come before—we would not have anticipated this explicit revelation: "He listens to the traffic on the highway and considers whether he should go to the basement"—and then the sentence surges, gains too much speed—"stand on the utility sink"—so far, a possible yet strange inclusion—"and hang himself with his belt." He is not thinking in the abstract, and we had no way to outguess the thought he was formulating because it does not logically unfold. "He understands he is willing to be dead." We had no idea this was at stake. Perhaps Leo did not understand, either. Perhaps, following his own thoughts, there was an internal emotional change analogous to a tonal change and—chillingly—his realization makes him able to step outside himself, seeing inside the same way the reader does, now. The last sentence might elicit a nervous laugh from us, since we're plodding along with Leo, and what does this guy in his undershirt *understand* that we wouldn't be able to think circles around? And then we get our answer. Time stops. The paragraph ends. Wherever we go from here, we will go knowing that the stakes are different, and that we were lured into something we thought almost ploddingly banal, only to find ourselves facing mortality.

No one could infer from Mrs. Nixon's conventional "Didn't she look beautiful?" that the stakes are as high as they are in the Carver story. But we can't make the mistake of feeling superior to Leo or Mrs. Nixon, both capable, in the hands of a capable writer, of catching us off guard. The premonition that we are willing to be dead is available to all of us.

Writing a story is different from telling a story, but if we omit detail while things brew beneath the surface, the reader usually picks up a sense of what those missing details might be, and what they might mean, by the tone. In person, you can tell if a storyteller is excited and connected, or perplexed and removed. We have the benefit of facial expressions, we often have a history that contextu-alizes the person speaking (as we come to have with writers whose fictional worlds we become familiar with), we're more in the world of theater than the world of prose. But a writer like Carver isn't going to stop to give you the character's expression (monotonous movement or the lack of it creates its own dynamic; Carver got this, in part, from Beckett), and he isn't going to jump to the point, either, the way our friend might lead up to a punch line. Carver is more interested in how one gets to that point, and he works like a camera, moving around his character, seeing from different angles. This technique is handled so subtly, though, that you don't realize you're moving with the camera's eye. You're in motion, and when you stop it's because you've been stopped the way Wile E. Coyote stops, suspended over a canyon's thin air.

Mrs. Nixon's remark about her mother's corpse looking beauti-ful hardly has the complexity of Carver's short story. As reported, it's a one-liner that really consists of *only* the punch line, com-plete with implicit instructions from Julie Nixon Eisenhower on how we are to react to her mother. But I don't hear it the way she has instructed me to, and I doubt many people would. You feel the tension, or even the terror underlying the emotion. She's play-ing *against* emotion. *Breezy* was a word of the period. You don't hear it much anymore. Mrs. Nixon was being a bit breezy when she phrased her statement as a question. She wanted to get away as quickly as possible—away from the people she addressed, as well as from the upsetting reality of the situation. Interesting that she married a man who could leave almost nothing untouched, rethinking everything, playing devil's advocate with himself (or any angels who might be converted), always second-guessing both real and imaginary adversaries.

She married a man who shared her anxiety about expressed

emotion: he arrived at ideas and conclusions (those times he ever arrived) by dissembling, hypothesizing, imagining stories that would be told, rather than getting as close to the story as he could and elucidating its substance. He believed everything in the world could shift at any moment. This is not a little boy to whom you would have wanted to give an ant farm. When he had the power, he insisted upon being the camera, making his audience move. He used words to superimpose one story on top of another. By the time he had concluded his half thoughts and ellipses, his curses and his hypothetical scenarios, he'd shaped a ball of twine into a cat's cradle so dense, even he could not escape. We needn't make him analogous to Carver's Leo, with his wife offstage, unable to witness his realization that he is willing to be dead. But in David Frost's famous TV interview of March 1977, we find out that Nixon, forced by the press's vigilance about the Watergate break-in and Americans' increasing desire to lay the blame at someone's feet to ask for Ehrlichman's resignation, told his faithful subordinate he'd hoped he wouldn't wake up that morning. If we trust this particular narrator, Nixon was willing himself to be dead.

The Faux Pas

Mrs. Nixon is quoted in Joe McGinniss's book: "Our group used to get together often. Of course, none of us had much money at the time, so we would just meet at someone's house after skating and have food, a spaghetti dinner or something of that type, and then we would sit around and tell stories and laugh. Dick was always the highlight of the party because he has a wonderful sense of humor. He would keep everybody in stitches. Sometimes we would even act out parts. I will never forget one night when we did *Beauty and the Beast*, Dick was the Beast, and one of the other men dressed up like Beauty. This sounds rather silly to be telling it now, but in those days we were all very young, and we had to do home entertainment rather than go out and spend money. We used to put on funny shows. It was all good, clean fun, and we had loads of laughs."

We might all, writers included, wonder: Did they know the story of Beauty and the Beast so well that they didn't consult the text? What fairy tale might people know now that would allow them to put on a performance without referring to a book? Where did the costumes come from or, if they were improvised, out of what? How was it decided that two men would have the starring roles, and was one of them embarrassed to be acting the part of Beauty? Did they just eat dinner, or did they also drink? If so, what? How much?

When someone is recounting an event, as Mrs. Nixon does, what impulse is it that makes a person conclude her story by giving last-minute information, as if we might otherwise misunderstand? Do storytellers assume they can manage the response of the listener or reader by deciding, themselves, on an explanation of the meaning of the story? Are writers ever off duty, or, as listeners or readers, are they always sleuthing for what's between the lines? When Mrs. Nixon concludes, is she rationalizing? Or just more grown-up, with distance from that scene? Would she like to be back in that room, watching that performance? If she could go back in time, what might have changed for her? Why do so many writers like ending on a note of ambiguity, whereas people telling each other stories like to make the meaning of the ending explicit? Why do writers resist believing that stories can be summed up, and instead take in whatever text they're presented with from a distance, skeptically, on second reading?

Mrs. Nixon's statement has enough specificity to be believable. Why do writers want so much more from stories than the literal level? Can this story be understood very differently from the way the storyteller reports and makes sense of it? However that question is answered, how much does it matter that someone who went on to be President of the United States was central to the story? How much does it matter that his wife is also a public figure? Are there stories that could be told about the past that could be described as the opposite of "good, clean fun"? If so, how might we get them? Could this story be the same without the mention of money? Did the usually recalcitrant Mrs. Nixon tell this story in response to something, or because it was a night she'd long remembered? If Mrs. Nixon could tell this story again, would this still be the version she'd want told for posterity? Does this sound like a recited story, or a written story? What would be the difference between the two? Do we assume that Mr. McGinniss quoted Mrs. Nixon exactly, or might he have cleaned up the quote? What happened when the laughter ended?

When campaigning on television was quite new, and the stakes were certainly higher than they were when playing a game in someone's living room, Mrs. Nixon once made a mistake on camera. Questioned by Bud Wilkinson and Paul Keyes, "She answered a couple of Wilkinson/Paul Keyes questions of less than monumental importance, and then, as the audience—on cue—applauded, she grinned and . . . began to applaud herself." Joe McGinniss, in *The Selling of the President 1968*, continues: "It was simply a reflex. There had been so much applause in her life. Going all the way back to the days of Beauty and the Beast. And all through this campaign. She had sat, half listening, then with her mind drifting more and more as the weeks and speeches passed so slowly into one another. Bringing her finally to this television studio on this final night where all that was left of her was reflex: you hear applause—applaud." She then made a second mistake when she realized what she'd done wrong and put her hands over her eyes.

The scene conjures up "Hear no evil, see no evil, speak no evil." It's probably true that Mrs. Nixon's mind was wandering, so whatever she heard (even if it had been "evil") was only half understood. Sitting in front of television cameras, you see nothing of the broadcast, only the cameras and the shapes of the cameramen. You're made myopic, cut off from really seeing the larger scene. The mistake was in congratulating herself, in responding to a verbal cue, and therefore being robotic. For someone as closemouthed as Mrs. Nixon, who you wouldn't assume would blurt out anything, the problem was not so much making a sound as it was being caught not thinking, not realizing that she was the center of attention, and that, therefore, good manners required that she not congratulate herself. Embarrassed, she raised her hands to cover her face, compounding the problem. The cameras moved away from her. Only if you wanted to do in your subject would you have the cameras linger—as they undoubtedly would, now.

Major and Minor Events
of Mrs. Nixon's Life

Working hard on the family farm in California, along with her
    mother, father, and two brothers

Losing both parents when she was young

Having ambition and trying to accomplish meaningful things

Having the courage to go on adventures, such as driving an
    elderly couple cross-country to their destination, and
    changing a flat tire along the way

Gardening

Sewing

Doing domestic chores

Graduating from college

Being robbed at gunpoint in a bank where she worked

Acting

Not marrying Mr. Nixon

Marrying Mr. Nixon

Having two daughters

Appearing on TV without a fur coat while Mr. Nixon
    explained to the nation where their money came from, and
    where their money went. (This was known not as the Cloth

Coat speech, but as the Checkers speech—their dog being more likely to elicit sympathy than a woman unadorned in fur.)

Traveling the world: to fifty-three nations, and to Peru twice (Mr. and Mrs. Nixon were spit on during the first Peru trip, when an angry mob tried to overturn their car. The second time she went to Peru, Mr. Nixon did not go with her. No one attacked the car.)

Making a decision not to express her views publicly

Advising Mr. Nixon to destroy the tapes

Yearning for vacations but usually staying home

Working as her husband's unpaid secretary ("Miss Ryan")

Disguising herself to walk undisturbed in Washington (usually at night, a scarf covering her head)

Serving as First Lady:

Giving tours

Ordering "the Nixon china," as her predecessors had ordered "the Kennedy china," et cetera.

Having spotlights installed to light the White House at night

Consulting curators about acquiring antiques, and repositioning existing furniture

Standing in receiving lines

Attending performances

Attending religious services

Inviting Jacqueline Kennedy and her two children back to the White House

Answering great quantities of mail written to her

Posing for her official portrait by Henriette Wyeth Hurd

Calling off production of "the Nixon china"

Leaving Washington for California when Mr. Nixon resigned

Reading Woodward and Bernstein's *The Final Days,* which her
 husband felt hastened her death
Arranging a surprise party for her depressed husband
Having a stroke, whose effects she worked hard to reverse

Mrs. Nixon, Without Lorgnette

Chekhov's "The Lady with the Little Dog" is known to every serious reader of the short story. It's a love story, it's eloquent, it's about yearning and what the aftermath of yearning might be—though Chekhov ends his story before we see the exact repercussions. At Yalta, a beachside resort, a married man meets a married woman, and the two become lovers. She leaves, but he cannot forget her. He eventually follows her to Moscow. He appears at the theater, where she is watching a play, *The Geisha*. He says hello, she is startled but quickly responds to his presence, retreating into the theater and eventually kissing him. Are they to escape their mundane lives, and are we watching the beginning of this—act one? Two boys see them kiss. No more is made of this. Anna Sergeevna and Dmitri Dmitrich Gurov—if one thinks romantically—are meant to be together. At story's end, at least for the moment, they are. They are, yet there is ambiguity: "And it seemed that, just a little more—and the solution would be found, and then a new, beautiful life would begin; and it was clear to both of them that the end was still far, far off, and that the most complicated and difficult part was just beginning." *The end* is ambiguous: the end of everything, death, or the way their relationship turns out? One interpretation haunts the other.

The idea of something beginning again, though, can weary one at this point. In any case, the reader can see that there is no more space and that the story will end with the paragraph. We have to imagine, but with imagining come effort and confusion, and what we envision is now tinged with portentousness: now that there is breathing room, the moralist (or at least the skeptic) in us can come out. It's almost required. We have been swept up in the inevitability, the *necessity,* of their union for much of the story, but when we have no more information, we can only imagine, and to imagine means to reassess.

Thelma Ryan, a.k.a. Buddy or Patricia, found herself in such a situation when she met Richard Nixon. He was compelled to pursue her—to go to Moscow, in effect—but I'm not sure if she'd lost her own sense of credibility, as has Anna Sergeevna, who wants her lover to respect her even though she has lost respect for herself. Sex isn't the issue: it has more to do with the idea of what one might become (and who's to know?), versus settling for a status quo of stagnation and social approval. Such liminal moments involve our sense of a future that both beckons as limitless possibility and weighs on us as looming necessity. Knowing what the future holds would simplify our decisions, at the cost of exhausting us with the knowledge that we would have to actually play it out, to read our own story to the end.

But what, exactly, does Dmitri Dmitrich offer? Early in the story we have this information: "In his appearance, in his character, in his whole nature there was something attractive and elusive that disposed women towards him and enticed them; he knew that, and he himself was attracted to them by some force." RN was hardly a lady-killer, but certainty—self-assurance—can be highly attractive, even in a person unsure of his desirability. The important thing is to act. RN must have understood that Pat Ryan was drawn to him, however much she protested, however much he did not fit her scenario for her future life.

Chekhov does not write the way he does ("there was something attractive and elusive") because he can't grab hold of the character. He speaks about unnamed forces because certain things escape being expressed in words. Arguably, such forces don't escape expression but rather hover as ephemeral realities that dominate by not being named. This is not some postmodern argument that all is, at its core, unknowable, that real communication is impossible. We can read everything touching on the life of Mrs. Nixon in a good-faith effort to see her from all available angles. We can research, empathize, let her coalesce in our minds as a believable character, and still not pin her like a butterfly on a specimen board. Rather than bringing her into sharper and sharper focus, we might see her from more and more angles, letting Chekhov advise us on reticence.

Perhaps most interesting, though, is this passage in "The Lady with the Little Dog": "Why did she love him so? Women had always taken him to be other than he was, and they had loved in him, not himself, but a man their imagination created, whom they had greedily sought all their lives; and then, when they had noticed their mistake, they had still loved him. And not one of them had been happy with him." Is Dmitri a realist, aware of himself in the larger context, or prideful and resigned to one of life's little ironies: what women do, how they become disillusioned, yet "when they had noticed their mistake, they had still loved him." It's difficult to answer because we don't know how he and his wife came to be together. If it's an epiphany, it's one he had earlier, not in this instant, and Dmitri seems to scuttle the possibility that life is full of sometimes pleasant surprises when the narrative continues "and not one of them had been happy with him." So: the women perceive one thing, find out it's another, then love him anyway, though no one is ever happy with him (in spite of loving him). And *that's* the status quo? Can Dmitri assume that *all* women see through him? Are we to believe that all women settle, in exactly this way? I question this not because of feminist sensibilities but because the assertion is at first strong and disarming, then perplexing, as a description of how relationships evolve. Again, we have nothing with which to judge this: not the testimony of his wife, not information from other lovers. The author leaves open the possibility that Dmitri tells himself self-serving stories that allow him to function.

Chekhov seems to write very directly, though his stories don't hit you over the head with a log; instead, they're more like persuading the reader to go gather wood. Chekhov tells us Dmitri "felt compassion for this life, [that of his lover] still so warm and beautiful, but probably already near the point where it would begin to fade and wither, like his own life."

These are the stories, even the moral lessons, by which we live. Reading Chekhov's story quickly, we might feel an intimate revelation has been made, and we should assimilate its wisdom. Read closely, there's every possibility that the narrator is fallible, critical but self-justifying, even if unintentionally. We are still hoping that "The Lady with the Little Dog" will have a fairy-tale ending—children and wives and husbands be damned, as always—but when we have stasis at the end, we can judge the characters only in terms of their words and actions, which here are not necessarily the same. If the courtship of Pat and Dick was left at such a threshold, we could project our own optimism or dread onto their untold story. Or they could tell us, confidently or disingenuously, what the future held in store, trying to control the stories of their lives.

Chekhov does not provide a moment of insight for Anna. Instead, she remains a character who does everything right, except for the one thing that she does "wrong." She responds to her frustration and acts on her desires; she flees the object of them; she reenters her former life and sits in the theater with a lorgnette, the better to see how someone else (*The Geisha*) lives her life of subservience. The first time we observe the lorgnette in the story, it is one dropped from Anna's hand; later, she has a "vulgar" lorgnette at the play (Dmitri's phallic projection). Sight—what one can see—is very important to "The Lady with the Little Dog." Anna's husband urges her to return home from Yalta because of trouble with his eyes. But we are blocked from seeing for many reasons, including the fact that some things just cannot be seen. Abstractions defy vision. Yearning cannot be *seen,* love cannot, certainly the future cannot—except in our peripheral or subliminal vision, perhaps, by the details that provoke the same reaction in the reader as in the characters.

Chekhov, in a letter to his brother, writes: "In the area of mental states there are also particulars. May God save you from generalities. It is best to avoid descriptions of the mental states of your heroes; the effort should be to make these clear from their actions." In the same letter, Chekhov writes: "In descriptions of nature, one should seize upon minutiae, grouping them so that when, having read the passage, you close your eyes, a picture is formed." Raymond Carver, who for many years read Chekhov daily, understood this. He placed his characters amid details, revisiting objects until their essence conveyed their importance; he gave us sparse details about the characters themselves. We don't think of a Carver character and envision that character vividly, as we do in Dickens. We remember that a character was wearing a belt because even that ordinary belt might have been put to use in an awful way. Carver had also assimilated the famous maxim attributed to Chekhov that if a gun is introduced early on it will have to go off by story's end. Details in Carver might be used or, more often, remain extraneous, like useless touchstones. Carver, of course, would never have a character offer an unexpected perspective on himself, as Dmitri does, with his ostensible explanation of how he acts, how others react to him, and what might therefore be expected. At the end of Chekhov's story, one character clutches his head while the other cries. We are told "that the end was still far, far off, and that the most complicated and difficult part was just beginning," which seems to unite the prescient writer with the character as perceiver. The author freeze-frames the ending but alarms us enough that we fear seeing things set in motion again. It is almost as if, in Chekhov and Carver, the story must end where it does for maximum scariness.

Those of us with vivid memories of the Nixon years might share just such a freeze-frame, remembering when Nixon stood in the door of the plane that would take him and his family away from the White House for the last time. Their actual departure, had it been a moment in literature, could have been a conventional conclusion—the end of something—seeded with some suggestions about how the future might turn out, but for me, this moment was interesting as it pertained not so much to the major character but to the minor. Whether we interpreted him as tragic, terrible, or any other number of things, for me, this moment provided a hyperawareness of Mrs. Nixon. What seemed mysterious was that a specific person had determined her fate—and how often does that happen? It was also done very publicly, calling attention to her in exactly the way she tried to avoid revealing herself. (This, of course, is something fiction writers have to be aware of, being neither judgmental nor cruel toward their characters, but also not avoiding painful revelations.) Often, writers say that, while they are writing, a character suddenly seems to be out of control (usually a good thing), or that, while concentrating on the main character, they noticed a face in the crowd and couldn't break eye contact—something like that. My eyes and my curiosity riveted themselves to Mrs. Nixon at her husband's side. I had accepted her as relatively unimportant; she was the antithesis of a role model; sure, I felt sorry for her, but wait a minute: who was she?

RN told himself many stories about himself. Most of them— the lies included—he was willing to have carved in stone. He didn't just read from a script that was written by his advisers or speech-writers; he worked on draft after draft of his speeches. For all I know, Mrs. Nixon might have been a storyteller, too, but I have my doubts because she rarely spoke for the record, let alone repeated herself, except in the most banal clichés. We'll never know if she saw through her boyfriend, then fiancé, then husband but loved him anyway (and was never happy with him).

Dmitri's last uttered words are a question. "'How? How?' he asked, clutching his head. 'How?'" The question echoes, catapult-ing the reader back to the point at which the lovers met, after which some inevitable force (perhaps only the writer) began to determine their story for them. At story's end, we have much information, but not all: that lurks just outside, and foggily infil-trates the reader's own life. The reader does a double take, imagin-ing not the characters' futures, as Dmitri's question suggests we should, but the characters' past, which we *saw* yet perhaps did not really understand.

We can easily imagine Nixon, and even Mrs. Nixon, in the days before the resignation, head in hand, muttering How? How?

How?, not obsessing about how to handle their future but projecting themselves back to the source, real or imagined, of their self-created tragedy. Certainly the appearance of Mr. Nixon became that point in Pat Ryan's life, the mystery to which every question returned.

Approximately Twenty Milk Shakes

As the gals know, drinking a milk shake every now and then isn't a bad idea, if you've dropped a little too much weight. Rushing around, traveling, volunteering, caring for our children . . . it can be a bit stressful, and sometimes you forget good nutrition. There's just too much to do, and you forget about the importance of keeping up your strength. If you find yourself altering your dresses, it might be time to get on the scale, acknowledge how much weight you've lost, and try to do better.

A milk shake is easy to make. All you do is take down your cocktail shaker and put in a scoop of vanilla ice cream, or whatever your favorite flavor is, and fill the shaker half full of milk, then add a tablespoon of flavoring, such as Hershey's chocolate syrup. Then shake away, and pour your milk shake right into a big glass and enjoy it. It's festive, pretty, and full of calories.

We girls aren't the only ones who can benefit from a "milk shake boost." My husband has recently been running for political office, and the television—which is rumored to add weight to your image—turned out not to be his friend! Also, he'd let the makeup person use "shave stick" on his beard, which only made it worse.

He was debating a robust-looking and, some would say, handsome man, John F. Kennedy. Mr. Kennedy has a full face to begin with, and his makeup person seemed to do the right thing—and also he doesn't have the heavy beard Dick has. In any event, our physician, Dr. John C. Lungren, took me aside. "Pat," he said, "Dick looked rather puny on television. You can see his hectic schedule has taken a toll. I think he'd do well to drink a milk shake now and then." I agreed with him, and then I found out exactly how many milk shakes he wanted me to prepare for Dick. It was four a day! We had from October 8 until October 13 to put some weight on Dick, and I began my milk shake making right away. A man doesn't mind a chocolate milk shake, let me tell you! No sooner had I hung up the phone than I interrupted Dick, letting him know the doctor's plan. Then I went out and got the ingredients and came home and scooped and shook. I think Hershey's makes a lovely, rich chocolate sauce, so I punched the can in two places (which makes it flow more easily) and put in a little more than a tablespoon, and I shook the shaker until I felt everything was blended, and then I got a large glass and poured in the thick mixture, then carried it in to Dick. He was still fretting about the debate the night before, Mr. Kennedy saying that we should apologize to the Russians for the U-2 spy plane incident. Dick feels we should never apologize when we're doing the right thing to defend our country. I agreed with him again and handed him his milk shake. I didn't tell him that he should be drinking four a day, because then it might have seemed like a chore rather than a treat. Several hours later, when he was on the phone, I just put another milk shake in front of him, and though he looked surprised, when I passed by his door later, I saw he'd taken a few sips.

At dinner I told him, "Dick, Dr. Lungren thought you looked too pale and thin on television, and we don't want people to have that impression, so he's come up with a plan for you to drink a number of milk shakes every day before the third debate." We already knew the makeup had made his beard look worse, so that was going to be changed.

"Pat," he said, "how many milk shakes are we talking about?"

"Four," I said, honestly. "And if you drink two more today, you'll have had at least twenty milk shakes, and will have gained a bit of weight before you see Mr. Kennedy again."

"Apologizing to the Russians would make us look weak!" he said. He was really very upset about Mr. Kennedy's proposed solution to Mr. Powers's plane being shot down.

"Dick," I said, "be that as it may, I will bring you milk shakes four times a day, and you can have the last one before bed."

"What if I miss out on sleep, getting up to pee?" he wanted to know.

I told him that I would give him the last milk shake half an hour before bed.

This is what we did, from October 8 to 12, and on the morning of the thirteenth, he drank a final milk shake before leaving for the studio. I reported to Dr. Lungren that we had executed his plan, and I know he was pleased. Also present were Dr. Malcolm Todd and Dr. Hubert Pritchard, who were there to brief Dr. Lungren on Dick's knee infection and his stay at Bethesda Naval Hospital.

Dick did well in the debate and looked better on television, in my opinion. The milk shakes were chocolate, except for my presenting him with one strawberry, for variety. It was an easy way to prepare his "prescription" milk shakes.

Rinsing immediately afterward keeps you from having to immerse the cocktail shaker in soapy water.

Friendly, Faithful, Fair

As a young woman, Buddy was busy taking care of the house, cooking, and cleaning, before and after her parents died. There was always very little money. Pleasures were few, and those were intermittent and small: when her father had money, he occasionally bought her a strawberry ice cream cone. She worked when she went to college—among other places, in a bank, where she was both a teller and a floor cleaner. She was always busy, and she had no objection to hard work. She had a lot of energy, but people with energy can also be self-indulgently lazy, so we can't draw too tidy a picture here. She had ambition, but that can be even more problematic than energy: ambition dissipates, does not necessarily prosper by being thwarted, devolves over time into other ways of achieving things. She yearned to travel, and in 1934 went by bus to Niagara Falls—a forerunner to Princess Di going alone to the Taj Mahal. We have no shoe box filled with her childhood memorabilia under the bed, no drawings, poems, or even report cards. At one point or another—often when young—people usually write a few poems. I have no idea if she ever wrote one. What come to mind are the rare occasions when Mrs. Nixon expressed herself quite tersely and sarcastically, being nobody's fool. Again like Princess Di, she was drawn to the sick and needy. She did work nursing patients, and she preferred seeing schoolchildren to seeing politicians, as who would not. She sewed curtains and slipcovers for the houses the Nixons rented or bought. Many people rolled their eyes about her pressing her husband's trousers. More people rolled their eyes about her "respectable Republican cloth coat," but this was her husband's term, not hers—and eventually there were plenty of photographs of her attired in fur. She was not averse to sitting with fur flung over her on a cold day, and was willing to share with her friend Mamie Eisenhower. Julie Nixon Eisenhower recounts: "In the bitter cold of the football stadium Mamie and Pat huddled shoulder to shoulder, the future First Lady's warm white-fox fur draped protectively over both."

She once walked some distance to the house of a friend, the wife of Senator Stennis, tromping through the snow in order to go to tea, carrying her shoes in a bag. There is nothing wrong with being practical, which she seems always to have been. While her husband was fanatically concerned with appearances, she seems not to have shared his concern. Neatness was necessary. She liked to have a pleasant environment, but small comforts pleased her, and she never cared about acquiring anything just because it conferred status. She selected her wardrobe primarily on the basis of what would pack well. As First Lady, she did travel with her hairdresser. She kept things, including herself, neat, all her life. She rolled bandages with a group of other women, and we can assume she did it carefully.

She was given a present in June 1960, by an appreciative group called "The Ladies of the Senate," whose bestowal Julie includes in *Pat Nixon: The Untold Story*. Probably there was a written record of the ceremonial speech, because otherwise, how could Julie, who was not present, know? It does not seem like a speech Mrs. Nixon would have remembered distinctly, nor did she ever, in telling a story, speak of herself as "Pat Nixon," though her husband often referred to himself as "he" or "the President." Here is Julie's account of Mrs. Nixon receiving her present:

Pat Nixon, we have a gift for you. It is a crystal bowl. We chose this because it was crystal clear eight years ago when you became the president of our group here, we liked you. Later on it was crystal clear we loved you, and we still do. You are friendly, faithful, and fair.

You are friendly, irrespective of party or age. You are faithful, far beyond the call of duty. You are fair, adding beauty to our interior decoration!

You have a rare and heartwarming quality of making everyone you greet seem more important than yourself.

Our gift is a crystal bowl, not a crystal ball. You won't be able to see into the future, but we hope you can see clearly into the past, and how much happiness you have brought us. Great happiness to you, Pat Nixon, and God bless you.

She might have been thrilled. She might have taken the bowl home and written a poem about it, or the gift might have provoked her to read Keats's "Ode on a Grecian Urn" and ponder the word *fair*. It's a conventionally structured speech in which words were judiciously selected and used to make a nice turn of phrase. We move from "liked" to "loved." This is because the recipient of the love has been *friendly, faithful, and fair*. These words stand out because of their meaning, because they alliterate, and because they have a job to do. They are emphasized for being set apart from the other words in their appearance, just as Mrs. Nixon's physical appearance has brought the ladies much delight. And they have given thought to the gift—a conventional present but here imbued with specific meaning for what it is not as well as for what it is. "Crystal bowl" versus "crystal ball" lets us see how close, yet how distinct, these two objects are. This crystal ball is unusual in that it might provide a look into the past rather than the future.

The past was always catching up with Mrs. Nixon, whether or not she had their gift to gaze into. When she had freedom, it was in the past: when she married a politician, her freedom was curtailed. Things were decided for her. She was summarized in the words of other people. Whether she had a proclivity for silence or merely decided upon it as adaptive behavior for survival, she was often silent, and that silence was unquestioned by the family. Publicly, she did not discuss politics but instead made innocuous remarks. Like so many people receiving a gift, she might have felt a mixture of pleasure and embarrassment at being singled out. There is no record of her response to the bowl. A writer could set that bowl spinning, reading into it as those who selected the gift did, imagining what image from the distant past Mrs. Nixon would have most liked to see: Her mother or father? The ice cream cone, as significant to her young self as Lady Liberty's torch? But you can't tell, when you look: she could have seen an English daisy, one she'd grown on the farm, liking not only its color but its durability as a cut flower. You take a risk when you look in the bowl/ball. Of course, you take a risk when you look in the mirror, or pass a store window and see yourself vis-à-vis the merchandise inside, an intruder in a winter skirt and jacket, standing in a window display of bathing suits, in the middle of March.

The bowl's presenters did not assume its recipient could see the future (that is just too silly, the stuff of fairy tales), but still there was a convention for suspending disbelief: it would be for a writer's convenience that a person could see the future in a crystal ball. Had she been an invented character in a fictional context, the bowl might not be elaborated upon when presented, so it could subtly and gradually become a symbol the reader could read into. Or everything that was said might be said, but by story's end the gift would prove to be something empty, and in its emptiness might be the expression of a greater emptiness.

In Hemingway's "Cat in the Rain," which takes place in Italy, the woman wants many things to make up for the emptiness she feels. Silver and candles are among the things she names. She also wants a kitty, a romanticized cat, something that is nothing like the uncommunicative, unempathetic man with whom she is trapped in the hotel room. The proprietor brings her what she desires at the end of the story, but it's a random cat, big rather than small, dripping wet and unappealing. He presents it to her as if the presentation closes the circle of desire. We see it's the wrong thing as well as she does: it's an anti–fairy tale, with romance unrequited; you might want a kitty, but what life hands you is going to be a big wet cat.

Just to speculate: What if Mrs. Nixon had wanted something small and clear, like a diamond? If this incident were fiction, the story could be constructed any number of ways, so that the engraved bowl could be as disappointing to Mrs. Nixon and to the reader as the moment when the wet cat was offered up. In fiction, she might have found the bowl years later and reflected on herself, younger, with different hopes and aspirations—someone who put the bowl away and forgot it, who was now finding either a more important bowl or one even less interesting. Things found years later can never be exactly the same. Again, I think of the widely held belief—erroneous but appealing to people—that Chekhov insisted if a gun appears in a story, it has to go off before story's end.

Analogously, if a bowl appears, it has to be used. But I don't know what became of Mrs. Nixon's bowl. We know that she hung paintings by Dwight Eisenhower in her home, and that after her trips abroad, there were many souvenirs, many reminders of the different cultures in which she'd traveled: large vases, Chinese paintings. But who knows where the bowl went? Who knows how she protected it on the ride home? Front floor on the passenger's side? Or did it nestle, again, in protective wrapping, inside a nice box? That would matter, in fiction. The writer would make that decision. A baby discovered, lifted from its blankets, is different from a baby already noticed at the beginning of a story, or a baby first viewed in its mother's arms.

As narrated by Mrs. Nixon's daughter, the words matter, and they say what they mean. But words are always altered by the things that exist apart from them that they cannot control, such as light coming through a window. The words will mean more or less depending on the light, transforming the speakers' intended meaning beyond their control. So the writer yearns to see what's been omitted, where the wrapping paper is, what pattern it had. Did the paper get ripped? Did she dig into the packaging? Mrs. Nixon doesn't seem like a ripper; she ironed her husband's trousers. But in this account—as opposed to fiction—the moment is gone. We could invent something, but we didn't get to see.

The bowl might be an accessory to the flash-forward. "Mrs. Nixon" would peer in with her own perspective, but since I know certain aspects of her future life now, as I write, I could interject a land mine's shattering explosion in Vietnam, or a person named Henry Kissinger, years hence, down on his knees praying with Mr. Nixon, or the Irish setter, King Timahoe—recognizable as an Irish setter but not yet as her dog—streaking across grass she'd have no reason to think grew on the White House lawn.

When writing about a well-known person after that person's death (or at least at the end of that person's life of significance for fictional purposes), the writer is largely constrained by facts. If not entitled to invent out of whole cloth, the writer can still imagine. The philosophy of Walter Benjamin is well known, but Jay Parini, in *Benjamin's Crossing*, decided to view Benjamin on the run from the Nazis, which the author can only imagine, for obvious reasons. Probably any fiction writer deciding to write about Mrs. Nixon would undertake a story that was not merely hers but her husband's. History is based in story. But where to begin, when she did not speak to the point, as a matter of principle, and the writer could only be tempted to project onto such an enigmatic person? Recently, Silda Wall Spitzer stood at her husband's side as he gave his resignation speech and inspired a skit on *The Daily Show*. In Mrs. Nixon's day, television had no Jon Stewart, no *Saturday Night Live*. People understood and more easily accepted that Mrs. Nixon was standing by her husband. Now, such standing by is suspect. We question the advisability of her actions ("Time will say nothing but I told you so"—W. H. Auden). By all accounts, Mrs. Nixon was dutiful and modest. She felt she had a role to fulfill. She did it unflinchingly, if sometimes teary-eyed, and left no record of her innermost thoughts. The bowl might have been passed on to one of the daughters. It might have broken, though we don't like stories to end that way, with such telegraphed imagery. Mrs. Nixon might have considered the words spoken during the bowl's presentation and come up with a few of her own: *polite, plodding,* and *pained.* No one inscribes a bowl that way.

But what about a husband who calls for a photographer to commemorate for posterity a family so sad and shaken by his forced resignation that the photographer found it almost impossible to take a picture without recording someone crying? Mrs. Nixon, obviously surprised, tried politely to suggest that their imminent departure from the White House, under a cloud of scandal, was not a moment that should be photographed. But no: Mr. Nixon had decided that it was a good idea. The POV of photographer Ollie Atkins would be interesting, but all we know is that eventually the picture was taken. Mr. Nixon was a man who knew how to pose and, in posing, tried to ensure that everything in his demeanor and facial expression, his body language, with his family an ungainly chorus line but nevertheless willing, even smiling, would suggest the way people in the future should interpret him, and his presidency. Mrs. Nixon looks animated, turned to the side, as if caught in an off moment. You get the sense she'd happily rise like Mary Poppins and disappear, if moving sideways to escape the picture frame wasn't enough of an escape. Mr. Nixon is intent upon giving the photograph his conventional best, crossing his arms to indicate he can't be touched, protecting himself while simultaneously suggesting authority, looking right into the lens with a big smile. Mrs. Nixon looks like she's already out of there. She's going toward someone, or something, but her eyes aren't on her husband. The bowl is forgotten, every insignificant symbolic thing is forgotten, she is trapped in the present as certainly as if she'd been manacled.

Her daughter Tricia, nicknamed Dolly by Mrs. Nixon, is the one who doesn't like interviews and won't speak to the press. Younger sister Julie is the family spokesperson, who urged her father strongly not to resign, having no idea what evidence of his involvement in the cover-up plot would emerge when the tape of June 23, 1972, was handed over. On the eve of his resignation, Julie, then twenty-six, wrote a letter to her father, saying, "I love you. Whatever you do I will support. I am very proud of you. Please wait a week or even ten days before you make this decision. Go through the fire a little longer. You are so strong! I love you." It is signed "Julie," and

"Millions support you." She had internalized what Mr. and Mrs. Nixon believed: that it was never an option to give up. This was to the chagrin of her husband, David Eisenhower. Tricia's husband, Edward Cox, simply could not speak to his wife about the resignation at all, it seems, though he was so worried his father-in-law might commit suicide that he spoke to people outside the family about Mr. Nixon's condition.

What sort of person would remember the bowl, in such troubled times, with the public watching and waiting? But, in fiction, what if she had just then stumbled upon it? Would it now be an omen, a symbol, an ironic mockery? What if, decades earlier, she'd kept the May basket her husband sent to her at Whittier Union High School (delivered by his parents' employee Tom Sulky), with her engagement ring nestled inside? She had thought they'd be together when she became engaged, but instead he'd sent it by messenger, unexpectedly, and hidden the ring in its box within the basket. She didn't like that: it wasn't the moment she'd anticipated. A fictional story about such a woman might relate the presentation of the ring to the presentation of the bowl, both being things that were meant as affirmations of something important. If Mrs. Nixon thought about symbols, weren't there times when she yearned to take off the ring? When she looked at her hand and thought, What have I done? How? How? How? Years later, after her stroke, she had to work hard to get back the use of her hand. The physical therapy consisted of using the afflicted hand rather than the functional hand. The theory was that if you forced yourself to use the weaker hand, you might regain its use. Imagine the struggle. Think of all the shortcuts people constantly take to do things with the least effort. The idea of not being a quitter applied unilaterally, so Mrs. Nixon practiced and challenged herself every day.

The day she accepted the gift of the bowl, she was in good health. She was energetic, accustomed to activity, an achiever.

As a fiction writer, I wonder: what could be known that the person, or character (Mrs. Nixon), wouldn't necessarily understand? Revealing these things is not a betrayal but rather the writer's admission of life's complexity, in which the central figure is sometimes the least informed, the most vulnerable. When Gatsby refutes Nick Carraway by insisting that the past can be recaptured, it is a sincere belief but untrue. (Nick, on Daisy Buchanan: "'I wouldn't ask too much of her,' I ventured. 'You can't repeat the past.' 'Can't repeat the past?' he cried incredulously. 'Why of course you can!'") We have to see through, and around, the character to see that things do not add up, or that we understand differently than the character does. If Mrs. Nixon had the ability to look at "Mrs. Nixon," what might she have seen? (She did, after all, have photographs of herself to study, as well as watching herself on TV being interviewed, et cetera.) She probably would not have wanted to dwell on herself. Some things might have pleased her, such as her neat appearance. What she said might have sounded fine, because she was judicious in her speech. So given her televised faux pas, and her awareness of having been out of control in front of a huge audience, how aware might she have been that in literature characters can play out their lack of awareness for hundreds of pages? Would she avoid speech knowing that words could have connotations beyond her control, that self-revelation defies our intentions? Disguise can be exhausting and futile. In early life as well as later on, when she looked tired, no makeup could disguise her fatigue. When Clare Boothe Luce was served breakfast by Mrs. Nixon after her stroke, she made the remark that she could see no signs of the stroke, and Mrs. Nixon replied, "Yes, but I *have* had a stroke. You don't know the struggle I had getting back the use of this hand."

Given her distrust of words, Mrs. Nixon might have had some glimmer of the fiction writer in her outlook, for many of that breed are the first to doubt the reliability of their means. About Watergate, she said: "He'll never get any credit for anything he says on the subject anyway. I wanted him to just state frankly that he didn't know, that no one knows, the full story of Watergate." Because she realized the danger of words, she'd wanted her husband to destroy the tapes and had given him that advice early on. But she wasn't much listened to: she put up effective blockades with the press, and her reactions were so habitual that her family seems not to have seriously engaged with her, knowing in advance what her position would be and not having the inclination to do anything but accept it. Later, she was able to retreat behind a guard station and fence at La Casa Pacifica (though it was hardly that) and spend much of her time in silence.

In Delmore Schwartz's story "In Dreams Begin Responsibilities," the character, as a young man in 1909, has a dream: he has the opportunity to watch a movie of his parents' as yet unlived future life, and he is upset because he can understand that they might not get together, but even if they do, he is implicated in how their lives will turn out, and they will not turn out wonderfully well. The often-quoted lines from the story have to do with his increasing awareness of what the future holds for them and, by implication, for him. (He awakens at the end of the story—at the end of the movie—to realize that it is his twenty-first birthday): "Don't do it. It's not too late to change your minds, both of you. Nothing will come of it. Only remorse, hatred, scandal and two children whose characters will be monstrous." It's a showstopping moment that leaves the reader breathless. Mrs. Nixon didn't sit at such a movie and tell her future self "Don't do it." If she could have seen a movie where she spontaneously pushed away the basket she knew contained Nixon's engagement ring, might she have thought, It's not too late to change your minds, both of you? She briefly and tellingly rejected her ring, in the same way she eventually pushed aside her concerns about marrying and being tied down. "Nothing will come of it. Only remorse, hatred, scandal . . ." When the lights came up, she stayed in the spotlight right through the final family portrait before leaving the White House, then accompanied her husband on his rounds of saying good-bye. She was so choked up, though, and her staff was so upset that, unable to speak, they only squeezed each other's hands. That would have been the picture that said more than words: a close-up of Mrs. Nixon's hand grasping a staff member's hand.

There are times when nobody sane believes in words.

The Quirky Moments of Mrs. Nixon's Life

(Recounted by Julie Nixon Eisenhower)

A trip to Mexico with her longtime friend Helene Drown. Posing for a picture in a donkey cart, Helene wearing a sombrero imprinted "I Love," and Mrs. Nixon wearing a "Mexico" sombrero.

As part of her job as a saleswoman at a California department store, she modeled clothes for Walter Pidgeon and his teenage daughter. This took two and a half hours. Ms. Pidgeon exited with a new wardrobe.

Driving an elderly couple across country to make money, and being driven crazy by the man's constant clicking of his dentures.

On inauguration morning, the Lyndon Johnsons arranged a little joke, or something. One can't be sure what the Lyndon Johnsons thought. Somehow, they got the Nixon family dogs into the White

House. Julie Nixon Eisenhower narrates: "Lyndon and Lady Bird Johnson [were] waiting at the top of the steps. A few feet away were our French poodle, Vicky, dressed in a new white jacket trimmed in red, white, and blue, and Pasha, our Yorkshire terrier, his thin hair pulled back from his face by a ribbon. President Johnson sentimentally had arranged for the dogs to be the first to greet us in our new home."

Mrs. Nixon took a trip with Lady Bird Johnson to Scotland. Since there was no advance notice, officials had to scramble to accommodate the women. As a little joke, Mrs. Nixon said that Mrs. Johnson was "the President's sister." Asked if anything could be provided for them, Mrs. Nixon said, "Why, yes, we would love to have tea with the Queen." This could have backfired, but it didn't: the Queen was away at Balmoral Castle.

As a girl, Mrs. Nixon walked on railroad tracks.

As a girl, Mrs. Nixon rolled and smoked cigarettes.

Moments of Mrs. Nixon's Life I've Invented

(On the theory that facts can provide only so much
information, and fiction has similar limitations)

After her trip to Peru, where angry citizens stormed the
Nixon car, breaking windows and trying to turn it over,
Mrs. Nixon began a lifelong habit of taking a bath at
night. By the glow of a night-light, she poured bath beads into
the water and immersed herself. She ran her hands back and forth,
gently popping the bubbles. Only then would she lean back against
a plastic, inflated bath pillow, eyes closed for as long as she could
stand it before peeking to see if any tiny floating islands remained.

Several photographs were given to Mrs. Nixon of herself, to decide
which she thought best. H. R. Haldeman had noted: "All okay."
Mrs. Nixon was not sure why H. R. Haldeman would have been
consulted. There was no note from "RN," as her husband referred to
himself. A blessing. She favored two photos. As she was debating, a
vacuum started. There had been a dinner at the White House that
night, and the house was still being cleaned. Mrs. Nixon, in her
dressing gown, went into the corridor and asked the first Secret
Service agent she saw which photograph he preferred. Startled

to see the First Lady, he did not immediately respond. Several seconds elapsed before he said, simply, "Mrs. Nixon." She did not repeat the question. Finally, he pointed to one and said, "That one gets the brightness of your eyes." She thanked him and returned to her room. She looked at both photographs and thought her eyes equally bright in each. Why had it taken the man so long to respond? Had he simply been afraid to express a preference? Mrs. Nixon had trouble falling asleep. She wondered if the photograph the Secret Service man had rejected might not be best, after all.

At the beach, Mrs. Nixon liked to draw sea creatures in the sand with her big toe. She was also good at drawing the chambered nautilus. She thought anyone could do a starfish. She sometimes did octopi, though they were unlikely to be in the water. She was not sure whether the Portuguese men-of-war were in the Florida waters, so she continued to outline octopi, much smaller than scale. Her husband preferred the pool. Actually, reading in a chair by the pool.

She often hummed "Camelot." She had loved the musical, but of course Camelot had other associations. Robert Kennedy, after his brother's death, recited from Shakespeare, in his thick Boston accent: "And he will make the face of heaven so fine/That all the world will be in love with night/And pay no worship to the garish sun." It was Mrs. Kennedy who had called their time in the White House "Camelot." Was it Mrs. Kennedy, or had she just gone along with that?

Mrs. Nixon played a game with her grandchild Jennie Eisenhower. "Where's Patricia?" she'd say, covering her own eyes and lowering her hands with a sudden, surprised smile. "Where's Pat?" she'd say. "Where's Jennie, then?" she'd ask. Mixed up, Jennie would sometimes put her hands over her own eyes. "And where is the St. Patrick's Babe?" Mrs. Nixon would say, looking puzzled. Jennie would sometimes point at Mrs. Nixon, sometimes at one of her toys. "Where's the White Sister?" Mrs. Nixon would say (remembering having been called that when she worked with TB patients). "Miss Vagabond?" she would ask, drawing out the syllables but not so they would be scary. Her husband had referred to her that way in a letter, noting her love of travel. "Is Grandma in the room?" she'd ask, and Jennie would laugh, pointing.

Mrs. Nixon's Junior Year Play: The Romantic Age

A. A. Milne's play *The Romantic Age,* written in 1922, the first play in which Thelma Ryan, then sixteen, acted, indirectly spoke to her upbringing by being about romance versus reality, where reality is defined by domesticity. Milne's play often refers to *A Midsummer Night's Dream.* There is also much talk of food, and of the importance of cooking and of being in the kitchen. (Until her premature death, Mrs. Ryan baked pastry for her three children when they came home from school.)

Much is made of the character Melisande, whose unusual name (which the playwright seems to have fallen in love with, having the characters repeat it and discuss its bestowal over and over) has been given by her father. Her mother misunderstood what her husband said (as women often do in plays of this period) and thought she was agreeing to name their child Millicent. In any event, Melisande is called Sandy by her mother. Having many permutations of one's name would be familiar to Buddy, known more formally as Thelma Ryan.

The play is not so much about mistaken identity as about appearances. The odd Gervase (as opposed to the generically named Bobby, the spurned suitor), lost in the woods in his bizarre cape/costume, turns out to be more stable than his behavior at first indicates. We learn that he is a stockbroker. Stable versus a vagabond. He and Melisande get together, but not before she confronts him with her awareness that he is not exactly a dashing knight who has come to her rescue. He then confronts her with the reality of *her* life: housekeeping. Nevertheless, this being a didactic comedy, she is still his "Princess." Their union is going to work out (farewell, prosaic Bobby), and at the end of the play Melisande/not-Millicent/Sandy/non-Princess/Princess is in the kitchen, cooking.

Mrs. Nixon, very domestic, sewed and cooked for her family, even, as a senator's wife, ironing her husband's trousers until there was so much talk that this was de trop that she stopped.

In *The Romantic Age,* Mother is ailing—vaguely ailing—and has a crush on her doctor. In reality, Mrs. Nixon's mother, dying of Bright's disease and liver cancer, lived briefly at her doctor's house, which was not so unusual in those days.

In the play, the concept of romance is suspect, yet essential. "There's romance everywhere if you look for it," Gervase Mallory exclaims. The message seems to be: have your illusions, have them punctured, realize that conventional ideas about romance are silly, be more practical (while still in love), and reinflate as a woman presiding over her kitchen.

Interesting dialogue from *The Romantic Age*:

Gervase (showing the ring on his finger): Yes, my fairy godmother gave me a magic ring. Here it is.

Melisande (looking at it): What does it do?

Gervase (pointing to ring): You turn it round once and think very hard of anybody you want, and suddenly the person you are thinking of appears before you.

Melisande: How wonderful! Have you tried it yet?

Gervase: Once . . . That's why you are here.

Melisande: Oh! (Softly.) Have you been thinking of me?

Gervase: All night.

Melisande: I dreamed of you all night.

Gervase (happily): Did you, Melisande? How dear of you to dream of me! (Anxiously.) Was I—was I all right?

Melisande: Oh, yes!

Gervase (pleased): Ah! (He spreads himself a little and removes a speck of dust from his sleeve.)

Years later, in 1938, Mrs. Nixon auditioned for *The Dark Tower,* to be performed by the Whittier Community Players. Mr. Nixon also auditioned. Like any good young American, he knew about romance and knew the moment he saw her that he would marry Thelma Ryan (then not quite twenty-six). She was prescient only in sensing—as he sensed about his bride-to-be—that important things awaited them, but wasn't sure about getting involved with him. As we know, though she was never as smitten as Melisande, in the role she acted much earlier, she changed her mind.

Mrs. Nixon Plays Elaine Bumpsted, a Role Formerly Acted by Bette Davis

I n the play *Broken Dishes,* by Martin Flavin, Mrs. Nixon, then
nineteen and enrolled at Fullerton Junior College under the
name Patricia Ryan, had the best role, yet again. At least as
the prettiest of three sisters, and the one most often onstage.

The situation: Elaine (Mrs. Nixon) is in love with a deliveryman
named Bill, whom her mother considers beneath her. Clever and
intent upon defying her mother and marrying Bill, Elaine takes
the opportunity of her mother's and unattractive sisters' absence
not to do what she is expected to do (the dishes) but to persuade
her hapless father, Cyrus, to give the wedding his blessing. He, too,
feels that he should be doing the dishes; his wife, Jenny, has told
him to do them. She legislates the rules. It is well known in the
family that she married beneath herself. She is not kind. As with
The Glass Menagerie by Tennessee Williams, which followed years
later, we observe a delusion of happiness that becomes unhappiness as it boomerangs back. Women in plays of this period seem
to have many self-sustaining delusions that ultimately also punish
others.

Nice, naïve Cyrus is tricked and ends up giving permission for his daughter's marriage without knowing it, then feels obliged to allow the wedding to take place. The minister doesn't seem to know what is going on. He is deaf—ah, the miracle of finding a deaf minister just when you need one!—and, although his other senses are operative, he performs the ceremony while Cyrus, and the audience, anticipates what hell there will be to pay when the awful wife and her ugly, unmarried daughters return. This is *Cinderella* without the shoe; we strongly suspect the evil sisters may prevail.

But first, there is much running around by the prospective bridegroom: hiding (he breaks a vase), confusing Dad by disappearing and reappearing. The wedding takes place—the wedding gown, like the deaf minister, is quickly found—but thereafter Dad, who has had too much "hard cider," becomes ill. Elaine feels it is incumbent upon her to stay and nurse her father back to health rather than go on a honeymoon with her groom, who runs off too quickly—heaven knows, he must think this is how things are done in this family—then returns to reclaim his wife.

Home comes Cyrus's wife, Jenny. She had cautioned against leaving cutlery soaking but finds cutlery soaking. A broken vase. Teacup handles, too. It's all a mess, and we feel Elaine will not assert herself but rather stay in this matriarch-ruled family forever, though when Bill unexpectedly becomes assertive (he's been an aw-shucks kind of guy himself) and insists that his bride leave with him, he does prevail. Someone, we think, managed to get out.

But not before Elaine's big speech. She tells her mother that if there's wreckage in the family, it isn't the broken dishes per se but metaphorical wreckage Jenny has caused by being overbearing and self-absorbed. Just about then, a stranger enters. A stranger, but not such a stranger: it is Chester Armstrong, whom Jenny has used as a cudgel throughout her marriage, ever since she loved him as a little girl, and he ostensibly loved her. By the time he has become what Jenny has presented him as being (with his luxurious hair and diamond rings), it is because he is a con man, in disguise. He is on the run from the law, so he finds their house in order to hide (and escape through a window the minute the police arrive). Exposed as a criminal and a fake (including wearing a black wig; when Jenny knew him, he was a redhead who went by the nickname Brick, which, in this play, would seem, more aptly, to refer to Cyrus's mental state). He's gone again—leaving Jenny to confront the truth. He was never a hero: not hers, not anyone's. Kind Cyrus does not rub it in. He tries to smooth things over, so Jenny will not be devastated.

We are wiser at the play's conclusion. The henpecked husband has behaved out of character (he lies about Chester's presence to the police), but he has also acted to protect his wife. Elaine and her new husband find the courage to leave and start a new life. Mom has confronted reality and is humbled. The little lies by which we live have popped like so many bubbles of dishwashing liquid in the sink. At play's end, Mom dons her apron, in preparation for doing the dishes.

So: we have characters who are afflicted (the minister, by his bad hearing; Dad, by his obtuse good nature; the sisters, by their unattractiveness). Then we have the girl with gumption, ambition, cleverness, and beauty. She wins. Bette Davis wins, Mrs. Nixon (Patricia Ryan) wins. Men are untrustworthy impostors, like Chester, or kind (if underachieving) good guys: Cyrus is lovable and not quite up to the task of being a man. Bill stakes his claim to his bride and says he will leave town if she won't leave her family, making her take a stand. But it works out. We have to think that, even for Jenny, it works out, because her wickedness has been taken away from her; she will no longer be able to invoke the ostensibly handsome, perfect Chester. Of course, the audience has long ago been told to believe that people must face the truth in order to get on with things.

Broken Dishes was written the year of the stock market crash, in the period between two shattering world wars. The world was safe for democracy, and, domestically, things would have to be sorted out, too. Strong women were still feared, and presented as shrewish. Weak men were pitied or looked down on: real men had to govern the household as well as fight for their country. This is a play about a woman who, while acquainted with suffering, has spent her life taking the upper hand, punishing a man who is not the enemy (but who has not been her savior, either). Cyrus (an old-fashioned name, even a bit feminine, compared to Sam and Bill), like America itself, has to wake up. Cyrus has to seize the day in order to seize his life. But he does it so nicely, so protectively. He's a bigger man than he seems. He's the good, gentle American (if a bit silly), but he can be pushed around only up to a point. Elaine acts, while her parents can only respond. She could falter, but she does not. Mrs. Nixon's character contrives to marry the man she loves and leaves her parents—wiser, surely a bit humbled—to their new domestic arrangement while she and Bill embark on their new life.

Elaine's note to self: You're a clever girl, so use your wits; don't accept oppression; stick up for what you believe in; love whom you love, and demonstrate courage. If you act correctly, your actions will liberate others as well. Patricia Ryan's note to self: ditto.

When *Broken Dishes* was first performed in New York, on November 5, 1929, the *Evening World* enthused: "For one jaded by jazz, songs and music, there's a worth-while change offered at the Ritz Theater. And judging from its reception, the players will be jolly well tired of reading their lines before another offering gets a chance in the house in 48th Street. . . . Donald Meek [is] perfection himself. Received with fervor." The reviewer is suggesting that, though the play is a comedy, it is nevertheless substantial, entertaining, or informative to those "jaded by jazz." Things were being shaken up in the society, so the play can also be seen as letting the status quo get shaken up in order to reaffirm it. It isn't a "jazzy" play but rather typical: family life; an examination of the roles of men and women that also exposes the unhappiness caused by romantic delusions. F. Scott Fitzgerald, writing at this time, knew the same. Take away your illusions, and what do you have? Someone who has been brought up short, whose self-justifying lie has been exposed. And, folks, Jenny doesn't go out and dance the Charleston, she gets some humility. She does the dishes. Elaine, though—youthful, pretty, clever Elaine—seems to have managed to escape doing the dishes for all time. She's off, like Mrs. Nixon, married to the man she loves, believing in his ability to get a better job, to have a future that will be all the more perfect because she believes in him.

RN made lists when considering both sides of a question. Mrs. Nixon found one that listed the pros and cons, circa 1954, of continuing to run for political office versus doing what she wanted and withdrawing. She kept it as a souvenir and told her daughter about it years later. She probably kept it because it allowed her to point to the moment when things could have been different. But she'd already caved: pursued by RN, she'd given in and married him, though freedom had meant so much to her. In the play, Elaine leaves only when she has—*because* she has—a partner, Bill. We never hear that freedom, in the abstract, is important to her, though the attainment of freedom is a subject of the play. "Some convince selves (they are) indispensable—but not the case," a seemingly humble RN noted (his item 3) as a reason to aspire beyond the Senate.

Over the years, of course, he did come to think he was indispensable. RN had already passed from resembling Bill to becoming Senator Nixon, and was on his way to becoming President Nixon. And his wife always knew he could do it. It was just that she didn't want him to. She looked at the world as Elaine did: as inherently full of possibility, whether or not she saw it through the happy filter of being in love. The stand she had to take was against her own conflicting impulse toward being unencumbered, free. There was no father figure with whom to collude, no mother to oppose her. Some wondered about the man she agreed to marry, but her brothers weren't going to stop her. She said no to her other suitor, a doctor who'd proposed, because she'd never romanticized him.

You tend to be out there on your own if you're not a romantic. And in spite of her fond notes and little gifts to RN, and their rather spontaneous wedding, Mrs. Nixon's early life had informed her that there were no guarantees. She didn't have romantic notions about what life could bring her. She was determined to experience life, though, even if she did not subscribe to extreme behavior: domestic life versus flapper.

RN's romantic notion of himself was that he was a realist. Mrs. Nixon seems to have known herself better, and merely to have joined forces with this realist. She was hopeful, but not deluded. He stayed close to her, so that, unlike with Bill, there was no issue of his having to come back. He never left through the window. Though the law did come knocking, finally, and then he had to walk out the door of the White House.

Mrs. Nixon Gives a Gift:
Stories by Guy de Maupassant

A gift from Mrs. Nixon to Mr. Nixon, during their courtship: two books, to which he responded, "I have always wanted to read Karl Marx in order to be familiar with it. De Maupassant writes the best short stories the world has ever read."

Mr. Nixon dodges the issue of what's to be made of Karl Marx: it boggles the mind, the young Nixon receiving a book by Marx—from his sweetheart, no less, and during wartime. In thanking her, he stayed on safe ground, choosing the lesser of two evils to opine about Maupassant's stories. Since he goes into no detail, it's possible he really held the opinion expressed, though anyone who has written a thank-you note knows about telling white lies: who really wants a loofah, or a musical can opener?

Maupassant, a figure from the late nineteenth century, is remembered more as a writer of short stories than for any particular story he wrote. When read at all, his work is usually in an anthology. Now, he would seem rather didactic, with plots that teach a lesson. There was a time, though, when—as with every other occupation—the short story had a job to do. Part of that job was cautionary, showing people how their base desires might lead to disaster. Fairy tales pointed in the same direction, and with many of Maupassant's stories, one senses some of the same underlying messages—ones we've heard before, now directed at grown-ups.

Let's imagine that Mr. Nixon read one of Maupassant's better-known stories, "The Necklace." (I have no idea what story the Nixons might have read; I'm choosing an often-anthologized piece.) Let's say he found it one of the best stories in the world.

Mr. Nixon would have been reading a story about a man married to a woman, Mathilde, whose vanity and yearning define her. She is the opposite of Mrs. Nixon, who was not materialistic, and who lived in the world that surrounded her, making the best of it, working hard, but trying to have some fun. It was never very important to her to have a beau. She had an independent streak (maybe two brothers were enough). But—back to Maupassant's story—once presented with the possibility of being entertained and acquiring the accoutrements of social stature, Mathilde is immediately caught up in the prospect of having a really wonderful evening. Her psychology is so transparent that we understand she has been thinking all along about the issue that arises: she seeks to induce guilt in her husband that they have been invited to a social occasion which she cannot attend because she does not have fancy clothes. (This is a game women play with themselves all the time. Visa depends on it.) She protests that she cannot go, that the dress she has is inadequate, and furthermore—though her husband provides a new dress and raises the point that fresh flowers are perfectly appropriate as embellishment—she feels she needs some significant jewel to wear with her new finery. He seems sensible, though more than a little dull and easily manipulated; she is someone who has always had her eye on a more glamorous future, and she feels her discontent is rooted in her relationship with her insufficient husband. Mr. Nixon would never have proposed to such a woman. She is a type much feared by men: superficial, manipulative, materialistic, angry.

At her husband Loisel's urging, Mathilde approaches a friend who is better off than she. Might she borrow some jewelry to wear for the special evening? Done. Her costume complete, the evening passes without the reader really participating, since the characters themselves hardly do. The party scene is described this way: "She danced with rapture, with passion, intoxicated by pleasure, forgetting all in the triumph of her beauty, in the glory of her success, in a sort of cloud of happiness composed of all this homage and admiration, and of that sense of triumph which is so sweet to woman's heart." Stories used to tell us such things, in such language. They were stories *telling a story*. Some elegance in storytelling was required. So: we have waited anxiously during the time leading up to the evening; we've read an eloquent but controlled description of an ostensibly wonderful brief scene that sweeps us along (and out); then we spend time with the characters after the party. Mathilde, about to admire herself for the last time as the Cinderella she has briefly been, suddenly realizes that the necklace is gone.

But before this happens, there has been a brief scene—one filled with neutral descriptions that make it seem as if nothing out of the ordinary happens—in which husband and wife hurriedly exit the event. He worries aloud that she may catch cold; her motivation is to flee before other women realize she does not have an expensive fur coat, as they do. (One cannot help thinking of Mrs. Nixon's Republican cloth coat to come.) "When they reached the street they could not find a carriage and began to look for one, shouting at the cabmen passing at a distance."

Finally they find "one of those ancient night cabs which, as though they were ashamed to show their shabbiness during the day, are never seen round Paris until after dark." Even objects are personified: the cab has a personality, much like Mathilde's. Even cabs have a sense of shame at not being fine enough. Mathilde enters the vehicle, one contains the other, and—though she does not become ill with a cold, as predicted—she soon falls into a worse situation, having to make restitution for the lost, borrowed diamond necklace.

They work hard for ten years (a long time, in fairy tales), and eventually they have enough money that the necklace—or one closely resembling it—is returned to the owner. During this time, we understand that Mathilde and her husband, Loisel, have suffered and lost strength.

Ironically, the borrowed necklace was never real. It was "paste." The story ends with Mathilde explaining what happened to the woman from whom she borrowed it, who sets her straight and also expresses pity for her.

When Mathilde first encounters her old friend, it seems surprising that she decides to confess all. In the confession is also a kind of aggression, an insistence that the other person not be allowed to think things are fine when the storyteller has, in fact, suffered. This shows Mathilde's boldness: but while her confession is intended to exert her moral authority over the owner of the necklace, she only ends up being pitied. The wealthier person triumphs and, amusingly, manages to do so because someone of another class has misunderstood her, assuming that, if the woman is rich, she would of course have a real diamond necklace.

Moral lessons abound.

"What would have happened if she had not lost that necklace? Who knows? who knows? How strange and changeful is life! How such a small thing is needed to make or ruin us!" To the fiction writer the "Who knows? who knows?" is a more normative alternative in a parallel universe, a story often not worth writing. Most of the story is off the page, just as the necklace, itself, is missing. The important evening is discussed in one paragraph, so lushly writerly in execution that we wince. The ten years that pass do not take anything near ten paragraphs to recount. By the end, it is as if two disparate stories, past and present, suddenly collide, leaving the reader stopped at the moment of impact. Though at first it seems obvious that a moral lesson has been enacted for the reader, it's also true that no one within the story seems likely to respond to the wisdom of that lesson. Mathilde's character is set: her confrontation with the necklace's owner is not expansive but self-absorbed. Mr. Loisel (he has no first name) represents and maintains society's expectations. Madame Forestier, too, will no doubt go through life being Madame Forestier, seeming like a friend but really a bit inscrutable and, like her fake jewelry in its real box, not quite what she seems. She won't change. Things are working fine for her.

As readers, we increasingly see through the characters, yet there is no moment when they acquire insight and act on it to change their lives. What is said to Mathilde clarifies, but the clarification itself is a kind of punishment that cannot undo what has happened.

Those who think of this as an old-fashioned story would probably point to the revelation at the end that implies a lesson learned. Yes—but it's a lesson that, once revealed, won't do anyone any good. Did the Bad Guy (Mathilde) learn a lesson? Ten years are very real, and when time passes, it has passed. The last sentence, with its revelation that instantly interjects irony, rings hollowly, and nothing follows: "Oh, my poor Mathilde! Why, my necklace was paste!

It was worth at most only five hundred francs." It so rarely happens in life but so often in stories: someone suddenly announces a stunning fact, and is heard with crystal clarity, because a train does not clatter by at just that moment, muffling the final words. Nor does the character who is directly addressed make some rejoinder. In stories, people get their perfect moment, no matter how painful that moment is. It's allowed to be undisturbed, frozen for all time amid white space. The subject of "The Necklace" is power, and the story concludes with someone asserting power. The ending establishes the author's power, as well.

What might Mrs. Nixon have thought of the story? That it was about people in situations that brought forth one's worst imaginings? That a fairy tale, or a story with elements of one, has always been popular as a way for writers to take readers back to childhood, with the grown-up children just as eager to credulously experience the ride? Perhaps she prided herself on her common sense, confident that she would never face ten years of secret shame for a terrible mistake, a failed secret.

What if Maupassant had written a story about a woman who, perhaps against her better judgment, marries a man who promises to go places but who has a secret flaw, a sense of wounded pride. She is aware of his tendency to overthink things, to think of people as potential enemies, to speak in ways that may seem authoritative initially, but that often depend on devious strategies of entrapment. Yet she stands by him as he weathers a series of setbacks at the hands of those he comes to identify as his implacable foes, people he must undermine and destroy in order to survive. As his machinations become more obvious, she wonders whether he has always been defined by his own demons. He triumphs, but in battling his perceived enemies, he does something shameful, and harbors a terrible secret, one she sees, or wants to see, only in her peripheral vision. After his downfall, they remain in limbo, trying to repay the debt he barely admits owing. Might such a story have had experiential force, registered as a warning, or is fiction just fiction, a made-up tale? (Nixon's personal physician during his exile in San Clemente, Dr. John C. Lungren, writes: "Nixon's growing self-awareness would later deepen into dreadful self-recognition that would reach a catharsis of confidence during the seminal David Frost interviews of March 1977. As he confronted his own actions, the consequences flowing from his own fallibility would fill Nixon with great sorrow and deep contrition.") The moral— in both Maupassant's story and Mrs. Nixon's life—is undermined by the fact that awareness comes too late, that both women have spent their lives with men who will never learn the right lessons, will never change.

Short stories could hardly exist without the way power shifts within them. This is often, but not always, subtle, and balances are tipped incrementally. (In James Joyce's "The Dead," Gabriel Conroy, a complicated and hubristic man, comes to understand that his wife is, and has been, a person independent from him; he condescends to Gretta in assuming he understands the *essence* of things. He finds out that he does not. In Richard Yates's "A Really Good Jazz Piano," one friend is subservient to another, who *almost* gains awareness and asserts himself, though in the end both decide it is easier to remain complicitous and to play their familiar roles.) This shift in power might have been something Mr. Nixon noticed, reading Maupassant, if he wasn't too horrified to begin with by his worst nightmare, Mathilde. He would not have identified with Loisel, who worked hard but did not want to be noticed, and was henpecked besides. In selecting Mrs. Nixon, Mr. Nixon saw her beauty but also her reticence. This was not the sort of woman who would expect a diamond necklace.

I think Mr. Nixon appreciated her gift and wrote an enthusiastic note of thanks, but I'm not sure he ever read Maupassant.

One last consideration: Mr. Nixon gave her a clock and a paperweight. I suppose she could have chosen to give him a barometer and a shoehorn.

Mrs. Nixon on Short Stories

I f you want to see complications in a story, you can always see complications. Nobody ever said life was easy. One of the nice things about reading is that you can close your eyes and take a few minutes to think things over, while there's often no way to pause during a conversation and not keep up your end of things.

Works of art are meant to be stimulating, to offer different viewpoints, and to make you think. We wouldn't have the great country we have if people just acted on their notions without realizing that there are many other viewpoints to consider. From country to country, assumptions vary. That's why travel is so interesting—because you get other perspectives, and you see things done differently. You might travel somewhere and come home and find that you're not enacting your usual routine. If you've been to China, for example, you might return and try having rice and fish for breakfast. If you limit yourself to reexperiencing what you're already familiar with, you'll never grow as a person.

Fairy tales are a little like travel. Reading them takes you into the forest and off to the ball. In a fairy tale it's as if you're a child again, and you see things with a child's eye. When you read fiction, I think sometimes the writers want you to see things through their eyes, and I suppose it's good to go along with them and see what you find out, what they know that you don't, but just because they cast a cold eye on something, that's not the only way to see it. Your world doesn't have to become less cheery because some writer tries to convince you people are out there scheming or turning their backs on their fellow man. Sometimes you have to remember the bigger picture. Those soldiers at Iwo Jima didn't let each other down. And no men stopped Amelia Earhart from flying her plane, either. If we take pride in what we do, we're making the world better. Not too much pride, of course, but enough pride that our children can see that we believe in something and that we'll work hard alone, or with others, to accomplish the right goals. In some of the things I've read, it's pretty clear to me that no one has any real goal. Some of those characters don't seem to belong to any country, let alone to the family they've been born into. It seems to me quite a few characters have lost their way and either feel alone or make it a point to operate as if they're the only person in the world. It's pretty easy to sense when a crisis is coming in a fairy tale, but there's no telling with short stories. Suddenly somebody's just acting peculiar, and it's a bit upsetting. The Big Bad Wolf is pretty upsetting, too, because no matter what our age, we realize that certain people will always try to trick us. That's why you need to choose wisely and take your time getting to really know people, and making important decisions.

All over the world, people have the same desires. They want to be loved. They want to be warm and well fed and safe. Short stories don't often take that into account. I've read some that have made me wonder who these people are, they seem so intent on causing harm. It seems to me that a lot of characters don't really know how to go about things. There also seems to be a lot of unhappiness, if you read enough stories, and—maybe I'm way out of line, but I'll say it anyway—it seems to me the characters sometimes want to cause unhappiness just for the heck of it. You want to take some of them by the collar and talk sense to them. We can all try to do our best, or we can sink into despair.

I've heard that short stories are written to shake us up, so that when the dust settles, things will be a little different. Why would an author want to do that, though? Think about Cole Porter. His songs tell us something in a nice way, and he's clever, too. He doesn't write songs to tell us about some horrible betrayal. He finds a way to get across an upbeat message, so we feel better. When we're sweeping or cooking, how often do we recite a sentence of a story? And how many times do we sing some Cole Porter lyrics? That's exactly my point.

Certain writers, though, can make it seem like you're somewhere else and even somebody else—like Cinderella, on the night of the ball. I often hear people say they've been "lost in a story." We know we're supposed to get lost in a fairy tale, because so often one of the characters does. Some little child wanders off the path, ends up in the dark woods or something like that. If someone leaves the path, it's not quite as obvious in a short story, though sometimes you'll look up from the page and be startled to find you're where you are. Maybe you're startled by who you are, too. Stories are meant to transport us, but we should never let ourselves be overwhelmed with a writer's sad view of life and think we can't do anything to change our own lives. If that's the message, tuck the bookmark inside, shelve that book, and move on!

Caracas, Venezuela, 1958

So many angry people. They hate us. Hate Americans. That's the Venezuelan national anthem playing, and they are Venezuelans, and they want us to do the right thing and stand respectfully while it plays, and all the while they hate us. Spit falls on us, from above. Spit! Let them spit: it can be washed away, but their shame can't. Music, music. We stand, honoring their patriotic song, and they can think of nothing better than to spit on us, when we're here to represent the best country in all the world.

The girls . . . if anything happened to us, how would the girls get along?

They *would* manage, because they are smart and self-reliant and because people *do* get along. You do what you have to do. You do it hoping it's the right thing, but sometimes that isn't clear in the moment.

They'll get these terrible people in order.

(*Later, all twelve Secret Service agents would be commended for heroism by President Eisenhower.*)

Life involves danger. Every day, there is danger. You can't think about it, can't let that hold you back. If you have a job to do, you do it. If you need to express your anger, you write a letter, or you punch a pillow. That's what I've read about, in some of the same magazines that write about me. They advise that you punch a pillow, not your enemy! Imagine women on the bed, punching pillows! Anger only begets more anger.

(*Julie Nixon Eisenhower would later write: "At first the spit looked like giant snowflakes."*)

Moving toward the car. Their flag being ripped up. Ours. An angry mob, growing larger. They could have set upon us as we stood listening to their national anthem. They might still cause harm, but they are so wrong, so wicked, in the way they are going about this.

Flowers from a child. One must always accept a bouquet. One must always be kind to children. Little Venezuelan child, holding out her flowers. A lifetime of flowers for me, after all those years on the farm, where we didn't even have a vase. Or any time to plant and pick flowers. Thank you, little girl, with my smile, which is the universal language. It's not your fault, you've been told to spit, to be angry. Your parents are angry. It is necessary to forgive. If you spit, and if you then hold out flowers, I acknowledge not your bad acts, but your kind ones.

(*Julie Nixon Eisenhower: "The girl turned away in shame."*)

The wife of the foreign minister is sitting next to me in the car. I am so sorry for her, because even she is endangered.

Blockades. Dick's black limousine moving in front of us. Don Hughes is so worried: he has so much responsibility. We Americans accept responsibility and carry it on our shoulders like Atlas always progressing, however slowly. Those who seek to win by intimidation will not prevail.

Someone wielding a baseball bat. Dick's car stopped, being rocked. They want to turn it over, they want Dick dead, and all Americans to perish because of their beliefs.

(*Don Hughes: Mrs. Nixon "had more guts than any man I've ever seen."*)

Dick ahead of me in his limousine, me following. If something terrible happened to one of us but not the other, how would that affect the girls? Would the other parent always be the survivor that reminded them of the one who didn't survive?

Blockades. Like bumper cars crashed into one another. No way around them.

Heading for the American Embassy. We're told we're going to the embassy. Vernon Walters running back to make sure I'm okay. I'm okay, and proud to be an American.

(*Home from school, Tricia Nixon turns on the radio and hears what is happening. She calls her father's office. It is the first they've heard about it.*)

Imagine the embarrassment of the wife of the foreign minister. A pat for her hand. Pat pats the hand gripping the seat next to her. If I saw this from above, that's what I'd see: myself, offering a touch. What do they think anger will accomplish?

(*The night before, in the hotel: "Muerte a Nixon."*)

(*Andrew Marvell: "The Grave's a fine and private place,/ But none I think do there embrace."*)

Horrible, to sit and watch Dick's car set upon. Such a helpless feeling—though you can't give in to feelings like that, because we are so rarely truly helpless.

Windows smashed. Thugs. Terrible actions, if not terrible people.

Forgiveness frees us, when we'd otherwise stay clenched in anger. Sister Thomas Anna would understand. She would certainly understand.

These people are acting like a disease. I suppose they even want to *kill*.

Day after day, Aunt Kate tending all those people, suffering with tuberculosis. It killed Dick's brother. His wonderful, beloved brother. Hannah Nixon's favorite, maybe. I've heard mothers have favorites—though I can't imagine it.

The car is racing toward the American Embassy. Will they storm the embassy? How will it end, all this violence? *They* must have gotten hurt, too. Some of their police were tackling their people.

My red suit, a mess.

My own father dead of tuberculosis, too. So soon after my mother. In those days, you never said "Cancer." But it was listed on her death certificate: cancer of the liver. She couldn't come back to the farm but lay dying at the house of the doctor. And I sat by her side, and sat by her side, and sat by her side, trying to make it easier.

(*Cancer. A scary word, almost a cliché, when used descriptively. John Dean would later speak of "a cancer on the presidency," but on their trip to Venezuela, Watergate was an as-yet-unbuilt building. Even an unthought building.*)

They are thugs. Criminals. It degrades them, it does not degrade those set upon.

Julie, Tricia, Tricia, Julie, JulieTricia, TriciaJulie, both in my arms.

What I wouldn't give for a cigarette.

The Writer's Sky

W hat ways of treating a recognizable person are fair game when you're writing fiction? Both the writer's and the reader's expectations become complicated when the writer is creating a character based on someone familiar or—probably more common—if the reader can see in the character a mixture of familiar and unfamiliar traits, so that a whole new Literary Lego Person seems to have been created. Even people the writer knows are instantly altered when they are tuned to a major or minor key. Also, in the act of writing, the character can escape the writer's intentions, and come to dominate the story in a way that is unwanted (or at least unexpected). Freed from the restraints of real life, the person-become-a-character can grow huge. As you write, you watch your character inflate as if you'll be taking her to the Macy's parade, where her huge face will bounce as high as the treetops. *Containing* a character is often the problem.

Let's say the writer has a character who is based on a well-known figure—a situation increasingly common, as fiction writers struggle to remain standing in the Age of Memoir.

This development hasn't happened overnight. Our American forebears congratulated themselves from the very beginning for their nuts-and-bolts factualism, their rejection of fantasy, illusion, and fiction as unmanly and "just made up." Long before reality TV we prided ourselves for revealing the man, or author, behind the curtain as a scam, a sham. Such misleading trifles belonged to the old world of artifice, while we created a New Jerusalem of truth in a new world. Memoir or, as a friend calls it, me-moir, fits easily into our entire history, while fiction has always been highly suspect.

But what a change: memoirs now are usually about people no one would have heard of until they read the book, while novels increasingly invoke historic figures: Jay Parini's novel about Tolstoy's final days, *The Last Station;* Joyce Carol Oates's novel *Marilyn*, about Marilyn Monroe. Legally, a work of fiction can simply ascribe words or actions to a person considered a public figure. But there are few cases of writers bothering to write fiction merely to express a vendetta (graffiti is more effective), so the writer's fascination with his or her subject usually indicates something about the writer, as well. We also read excellent writers on any subject (William Shawn's belief, when he was editor of *The New Yorker*), and we are pleased when we think a writer is sure to have something fascinating to say about a subject we would not have assumed she'd be writing about (Elizabeth Hardwick on Herman Melville). When Edmund White writes a short biography of Rimbaud, we understand that there are two individuals whose stories will be heard: Arthur Rimbaud and Edmund White. Whether writers like it or not—they hardly ever *do* like it—readers have serious expectations of the writers whose fictional, or nonfictional, worlds they have come to know.

A certain class of writers—perhaps an ever vanishing number—remains reluctant to play to the crowd. In part, that's because the crowd is never right in front of them (when writing, at least) and is therefore unknowable. The writer can think only of his loyal dog, who never walks out of the room when he is reading aloud (he might hear the words "dog park" or "treat"!), or of his wife, who wouldn't dare, or he may have internalized the opinions of his fellow MFA students, who never think he's funny, or he might think he knows just the windup for the pitch to his agent, but in my experience, all people—even all dogs—drift away, in the moment of writing. The writer is left with herself as creator and merciless judge, struggling to keep left brain and right brain distinct.

Writers live an odd life, in which they face forward while spending much time looking back (*How much of this story do I know?*), appearing at enough events of daily life to stave off being served with divorce papers, while on a roller coaster of enthusiasm and despair, depending on how their writing is going. When you meet them, they often seem remote. That's because they're half in their fictional world, which they believe might blow away like a thistle in the next burst of wind (a wind, perhaps, from people recounting *their* stories, which the writer *should* know about in order to write something *really* interesting), and half fixated on passing for normal, which is the most difficult state to try to approximate. None of your clothes look quite right when your goal is to look normal.

Certain writers are energized by getting to do a pas de deux with a ghost. E. L. Doctorow's *Ragtime,* with its cast of historic figures, was published to wide acclaim and started a trend. Max Apple has a fabulous story called "The Oranging of America" involving the man who started Howard Johnson's. There are too many writers and too many dances to count, but among others I really love are Don DeLillo, entering the mind of Lee Harvey Oswald's mother in *Libra,* and Donald Barthelme's extraordinary story, "Robert Kennedy Saved from Drowning." The list of writers magnetizing subjects to them (or vice versa) is long; even posthumously, the character might find the writer, the way you sometimes dream things and awake with the spooky feeling that your dream was floating out there and came to reside in you, the dreamer. The writer may even be a most unwilling recipient. (We all know the danger of thinking that Cleopatra or Joan of Arc is talking to us; so rarely does the unexpected internal voice belong to the garage mechanic or the grocery bagger.) But writers can sometimes persuade themselves to join up, to experience unlikely partners. I am very happy to find myself paired with Mrs. Nixon, a person I would have done anything to avoid—to the extent she was even part of my consciousness. As a writer, though, she interests me. My curiosity is based on how little we share in terms of personality, or upbringing, or what fate has dealt us. She was a person of my mother's generation, who also lived for years in the place where I grew up, Washington, D.C., which was then such a different town (more Southern; less cosmopolitan; at best a shadow city of New York). Writing fiction about a real person tests my unexamined assumptions, letting me see if, in the character I create, my preconceptions are reflected, reversed, or obscured. It's an area in which I have a little (only a little) power—to animate a character against a stage set believable enough to transcend its artifice; to play out scenarios from outside my experience, limning someone dissimilar from me with whom I nevertheless empathize. Insofar as we know ourselves well, or are convinced that we do, that self-awareness also becomes our self-imposed predictability. What good would come of projecting ourselves onto the page: a character exactly "like" me might emerge, but that character won't offer me many surprises. Mrs. Nixon isn't *my* avatar so much as she's her own.

Years ago there was a book I loved, with photographs of a red sofa that was moved around from location to location (as opposed to the unmoving outdoor sofa plunked down in the projects in *The Wire*), context and object reinforming the viewer about each. Right now, while I'm writing, the "Sad Keanu" phenomena is being played for laughs all over the place: a picture of Keanu Reeves, sitting eating a sandwich, looking sad, that's been Photoshopped so that he seems to sit with a panda who also has downcast eyes, or to be sitting on the steps as Dustin Hoffman and Katharine Ross run out of the church in *The Graduate*, and Keanu . . . well, Keanu is sad. ("That's so funny," Keanu says to a journalist at *New York* magazine. "So they take paparazzi pictures and re-contextualize them?") I'm not the first to appropriate Mrs. Nixon. She is featured in a coloring book; eBay offers old "Pat for President" buttons, with a photograph of her smiling on the front: history as kitsch. And since she is one of only two former First Ladies in recent times not to have written a memoir, it was left to her daughter Julie to write "the untold story," or we wouldn't even have that.

Eccentric people, people who play against type, outspoken or outlandish people are pretty easy to write about. But what about Mrs. Nixon, who internalized the expectations of her time and enacted them meticulously (she took care not to smoke when she might be seen), or who also might have been shy, or more psychologically troubled than reported? Her youthful energy and independence were subsumed as she adopted her role as silent partner to a politician who promised her he would leave politics and allow her and their daughters to have a private life, yet who fought to stay in public office until the bitter end. I spontaneously recoil from any image of Richard Nixon, let alone tapes of his voice— and I resist reimmersion in the Watergate years, which provided the ironic backdrop for my graduate study (Wordsworth, Tricky Dick, and the Watergate mess, in the same summer?), but I have found Mrs. Nixon, the person standing near him (truly or met-aphorically), more and more fascinating. Am I saying that Mrs. Nixon found me? I suppose so. Mrs. Nixon is not someone I wish I could have had to dinner. I know perfectly well that she would not have confided in me, and I very much doubt that I would have asked her any direct questions, because—and this deeply dismays my husband—I almost never do that. I listen to what I'm told, which doesn't mean that I believe it, but I do factor it in.

I have my quick checklist about possible characters, as doctors do when they glance up as you walk into the office, before you've begun your litany of complaints, or as people do who are meeting for the first time after finding each other on Match.com: check the eyes; take the temperature (to speak metaphorically); do you instinctively feel some attraction? Being alert to what the person or character says is only part of it; you have to register what she can't, or doesn't, say. That's what I find intriguing to try to intuit. This was Mrs. Nixon's great mystery: not her resolve to avoid being controversial, but her consistent ability to pull it off; not her loyalty, but the sad irony of being trapped by what is in most circumstances a virtue. She was so obviously secondary to her husband—she, of course, enabled this codependence—but what is more interest-ing than focusing where your attention has not been directed, on someone who isn't the main character? (Years ago, I met Norman Mailer. He had left the party, as had I, to go into the kitchen and talk to the children and the cook.) So I began speculating about Mrs. Nixon, in part by researching her life and by drawing on my experience of literature. Consider:

In Frank Conroy's "Midair," a mentally ill father, who has escaped from the hospital, appears as a stranger at his children's apartment when their mother is away. He behaves crazily, up to and during the point when the people from the mental hospital come to the door to take him away. Most anything can be made up about your character, if he or she is crazy. That's one reason writers tend not to present clinically crazy characters; they'll always seem half credible, half unbelievable. Conroy writes: "For more than an hour they have been rearranging the books on the living-room shelves, putting them in alphabetical order by author. Sean's father stops every now and then, with some favorite book, to do a dramatic reading. The readings become more and more dramatic. He leans down to the children to emphasize the dialogue, shouting in different voices, gesticulating with his free arm in the air, making faces. But then, abruptly, his mood changes." I doubt that the reader would wonder what, exactly, Sean's father is reading, since his actions are scarily credible and the paragraph has to do with the general situation. Action informs us. Specifics can stop action. (Any specific reference to the books being alphabetized and read from could be made to work here, from *King Lear* to a book about astrology, but a specific reference would also be working against the reader's visceral reaction to what's basically going on.)

The father, being "crazy," cannot (or, at least, does not) express himself except through his actions, and, in the moment, neither do the children—being children—express their thoughts about what's going on. The story's brilliance lies in giving us the most dramatic moment first, and then, as the story progresses, we—as we'll come to realize the main character, Sean, has—forget the whole interaction. A moment of crisis in a stopped elevator much later in the story precipitates Sean's remembering this traumatic moment ("Midair" is filled with moments of suspension: the young boy, held out the window by his crazy father; airplanes; elevators), but by the time he and a young man who reminds him of his son are trapped together in the elevator, Sean has learned to be an adult, and his version of being an adult is to take charge—to tell the panicked young man, emphatically, that they can't fall. He is speaking at a great remove from the dramatic early scene in the story, but clearly its effect on his life is something from which he has never recovered.

The reader understands it all—in fact, the reader has always had more of an ability to analyze Sean than he has—but the errors of Sean's life cannot be undone, and his triumph of seeming almost unnaturally sane (really: *no* possibility the broken elevator will fall?) is undercut by our sudden awareness of how Sean is coping in the moment, versus the way Sean has coped, or failed to, his entire life. Like the old Polaroid cameras that had to be focused manually, moving the lens so that the double images become one, sliding two rectangular blocks with one superimposed over the other to sharpen the single image, the reader brings Sean into focus by overlaying the early scene with the similar scene that comes later. The Polaroid's layering is called "justifying the image." It works metaphorically to explain what we do, as readers, when we see the parallel elements of a story conflate. Had Conroy's Sean spoken and had an epiphany, however, the story wouldn't have had the same power. The tension and its potential resolution exist not as words, but as images. *We* have to see, and we do.

I can't take one moment of Mrs. Nixon's life and juxtapose it over another without pretending to knowledge of her intimate life none of us can have. She is now a historic figure, but while alive she may well have been unknowable, even by her family. In writing about her, I see her as a child standing on her parents' farm, which seems to be in the middle of nowhere. (Like Mrs. Nixon, even the town changed its name.) And then, in her teens, she is orphaned. Her determination to survive and to do well through work and perseverance seems to permeate any image of her from then on— supplying one rectangular block against which subsequent events will have to be justified. When I jump ahead to that future, and to Buddy becoming Mrs. Nixon, and then the wife of the President of the United States, my tendency is to bring her into focus by noticing the child underneath.

This is not the moment when you have to throw the book over your shoulder because I claim Mrs. Nixon spoke to me. She spoke to me as being indelible—as a young person, a figure in a land-scape—not by speaking words; in the many ways in which she withheld information (perhaps, like Conroy's character, uninten-tionally); as a person on the sidelines—always more interesting than the people on parade. People who are enigmatic, who don't give you a lot to work with, are more intriguing. There's no reason, though, to want to turn such characters inside out; in fact, the more potentially revelatory thing is to let them have their integ-rity, but not to be so intimidated or reverential that you forget to also play with them—to see if you can tease them out of their silence; to reveal them in their off moments. Some writers have a more systematic approach to character, while others are more at ease feeling that a character evolves, and that the Rorschach test is open to vast interpretation. There's absolutely no way to verify that you got it right, no matter how many positive responses you get, saying *Wow, you really nailed it*. And those times the sub-ject escapes, it doesn't matter if other people assure you that the subject's in custody. In my perverse heart of hearts, I applaud the runaway. Though I'm the one supplying the Rorschach, I'm always secretly delighted to know that the blot is not definitive, only taken by some to be so.

Writers I know tend to be superstitious—at least, about one aspect of writing—in that they don't want to describe what they're writing about in medias res. They feel that the energy will dis-sipate, or that they'll talk about it rather than write it, or that the book will change on them (it quite often does, and being on guard won't protect you). When I lived in a small apartment and my desk was in my living room, I threw towels over the papers on my desk before people came over. Others might hide the medicine bottles, but with writers, it's usually the manuscript. Therefore, I hid the many books I read about Mrs. Nixon from everyone except my husband. (One friend who walked into my writing room made no comment but later brought me a two-ton book by Bob Haldeman.)

When I teach literature, my reactions are very much a reader's reactions; it never occurs to me that what I'm discussing has the slightest thing to do with what I sometimes do (write). There's a system or world that requires me to discover *its* inherent logic, to learn to navigate by subtle signs (anything from punctuation marks to descriptions that might eventually suggest a motif). Every reader has to read enough (and to have read enough in general) to understand a particular writer's tone. The writer must educate the reader, yet writers can do this only if they're lucky enough that the reader returns repeatedly to that writer's work.

Katherine Anne Porter, considering Virginia Woolf, describes the writer's landscape by channeling her subject: "Life, the life of this world, here and now, was a great mystery, no one could fathom it; and death was the end. In short, she was what the true believers always have called a heretic. What she did, then, in the way of breaking up one of the oldest beliefs of mankind, is more important than the changes she made in the form of the novel. She wasn't even a heretic—she simply lived outside of dogmatic belief. She lived in the naturalness of her vocation. The world of the arts was her native territory; she ranged freely under her own sky, speaking her mother tongue fearlessly. She was at home in that place as much as anyone ever was." This assessment is inspiring, as well as astute. It raises the question: how many writers do feel there's a "naturalness" to their vocation?

Today, when writing has been taken up by the academy, writers are nudged toward a new form of self-consciousness (ask any MFA student); there are now numerous forums for delivering one's words aloud—a different test of the text—as well as putting them on paper. *Naturalness* seems like a loaded word—a lovely word (the *s*'s trail away) that connotes desirability, but at the same time makes me nervous and a little defensive. Any writer can claim certain territory by interacting with it repeatedly: the objective place becomes subjective, because the writer was drawn to it for personal reasons; Faulkner's South is different from Flannery O'Connor's, but once inhabited by both of them, the South will never be the same. (The setting of a work of literature has to do with geography, but of course that terrain can also be imagined: in dystopian literature, the dream is the nightmare.)

But that other notion—the idea that writers live under their "own sky." They *do*. In writing fiction convincingly, what they have to do is point to a specifically literary sky, a sky under which anything is possible, and move their characters through a landscape that's right for them, even though their scribes may live elsewhere, or prefer other territory. We could literalize Ms. Porter's metaphorical sky: when writers are absolutely integrated into their own landscape, and have chosen to place their characters there, they have a clear advantage (Cormac McCarthy, Annie Proulx, Jim Harrison), but for the many writers who grew up anywhere, and belong nowhere, the sky can't easily be invoked with conviction. I think that's why it's not often referred to—or is referred to with self-consciousness. The fiction writer tends to look as high as a tree, or even a mountain, but often the sky seems too much. Poets consider their sky a lot more than fiction writers. I wonder if the inherent constraints of a poem give the poet an impulse to look at something vast, while the many pages available to the fiction writer nevertheless suggest that the writer focus on detail.

Mrs. Nixon may have had her own sky, one she felt at home under, when she was a child, or remembered wistfully as she spent years under city skies, looking up through smog and obliterating lights. Walking under such gray skies, hiding behind a head scarf pulled over her forehead to provide anonymity as time went on, going out at night so as not to be seen, she might have felt the openness above her both as a vanished world and as a reproach. Her world really did begin to vanish in her lifetime, though her choices in life would have taken her far from that farmland in any case. She believed in facades, as well: she was the one who wanted the White House illuminated at night, its lights bright in celebration. Though she never wanted a life in politics, once she had it, there was no reason the ultimate symbol of what had been attained shouldn't burn bright.

F. Scott Fitzgerald, in "The Crack-up," writes: "Fifty years ago we Americans substituted melodrama for tragedy, violence for dignity under suffering. That became a quality that only women were supposed to exhibit in life or fiction." This was written in the 1930s. The notion of a woman's "dignity" has been somewhat rethought as repressive, though the number of political wives who have had to apologize for speaking out continues to grow. I don't think Mrs. Nixon would be surprised by the continued assumption that first ladies are to be seen and not heard. Remember Hillary Clinton furiously backpedaling after dismissing as unimportant the idea of baking cookies, and Michelle Obama excoriated for implying that she hadn't been unilaterally proud of her country every second of her life? Women are coached on how this is done—how they can say two seemingly contradictory things at the same time, and be true to no one, including themselves—in order to come clean and make amends on *The View*.

The view, indeed: depending on who you are, where you stand, and whether you've got the chutzpah to stare down the sky.

Mrs. Nixon Considers Automatic Writing

The idea is that you pick up a pen and just start writing. Can you imagine? If you saw a thread dangling from your hem, would you pull it and keep unwinding and unwinding until the skirt became a miniskirt, and then nothing but a waistband? If you did, what would you have except something you'd destroyed and couldn't wear?

The Letter

Richard Farnsworth smiled good-bye to the secretary and strolled out of the office, a piece of stationery tucked in his briefcase. John Hayes, his boss, tended to be suspicious of his employees, especially if he thought there might be any romance going on. At the office Christmas party, he'd stood like the former soldier he was when his own wife came in late and threw her arms around him. If you knew John, you could have seen a tiny gleam of pleasure flicker in his eyes, though, as he'd handed her a cup of punch. The office was all about business, and Richard worked hard and wanted to do well—at least as well as he'd done at Princeton.

"Mr. Farnsworth," Belinda, the secretary, called after him, as he was walking down the stairs. "Mr. Farnsworth, would you have time to sign this letter?"

He walked back to the doorway, where she stood smiling inquisitively. Belinda Hayes had just graduated from school and come to work in her father's office. She had golden hair and smiling cheeks. She was a clever girl, so she might have known that quite a few men in the office admired her beauty, but would not dare approach because she was the boss's daughter. He took the

fountain pen she handed him and put his signature on the document, practicing trailing the final *h* of his name into a little upward
turn, like a check mark approving his own name.

This was the afternoon he had long been waiting for, through
the long winter with snow that piled up everywhere like reams of
untouched typing paper. It was not Belinda Hayes, however, to
whom he wanted to dedicate the novel he was planning to write.
It was his best friend Bill's sister, Harriet Reese Miller, who had
returned from summer camp the day before, and called Richard
just as she'd promised she would.

Harriet Reese Miller, at eighteen, was too old for summer camp,
but she loved it so much that the owner of Camp Walla-Wahee
had arranged for her to return as a counselor. Though Richard had
never seen her in a bathing suit, he imagined her dressed in one
every night before he fell asleep, a black bathing suit that drew
attention to her beautiful swan neck, with a white band that accen-
tuated her slim waist and provided a clear indication that she was
mostly girl and just a little bit swan.

The street ahead was lined with buildings where angels peered
from pilasters and columns supported impossibly heavy weights,
like performers whose act involved standing stock-still. It was the
act performers wanted you to notice, not them, because they were
mere instruments of transformation. He looked at the sky and saw
the clouds slowly drifting, like sentences trailing other sentences,
growing wispy and evaporating if they were not recorded. He
should be writing his book, he knew that, but he needed a job so he
could save the money to marry Harriet, and when that book was
closed, when she was his very own, he would have the courage to
take on anything in the world. He noticed, again, the Corinthian
column, with its ornate top, and patted his hair to make sure he
looked neat, stood upright because rising an inch higher made him

feel a bit more powerful. He had learned from his boss's manner, without being told.

He went to a florist's and gazed at the flowers, imagining them as a bouquet Harriet would hold in front of her, walking slowly toward the altar. But today he could pick only one, the perfect flower for the most beautiful girl. He considered Queen Anne's lace, but his love was an all-American girl, so he decided that was too regal. And if a rose by any other name would smell as sweet, perhaps it would be more imaginative to select something other than a rose? "Does she have a favorite color?" asked the perky young woman behind the counter. Of course! Her favorite color was . . . well, it might be pink. He had never asked, he realized. He remembered the white belt of her bathing suit and decided white might be better. White suggested purity, but also conjured up his secret vision. He pointed to a vase that contained a stalk of something whose name had as many syllables as his heart had constant thoughts of her. The flower was called "delphinium," and it had many, many blossoms all the way up its tall stalk to the still tightly closed tip, which, too, would flower as time went on. It was carefully wrapped in a cone of lavender paper and tied with a pale green ribbon, whose ends were made to curl into happy confusion as the young woman ran a scissors over the tips.

Back on the street, he walked until he turned in to the park where she said that she would meet him. He was early, because choosing the flower had not taken as long as he'd anticipated, but still he had to write his note. He wanted it to have the immediacy of something deeply felt, but also seem to have been written spontaneously. One of his fears in embarking on his other project, his book, was that so much time would be spent that in every word one might hear the ticking of the clock. He had spoken to no one but Harriet about his dream of being a writer. He would write their love story, but it would be one that took place in the future, without time passing and parents hovering and the obligations of the office swarming him like worker bees surrounding the queen. Their story would reveal itself as the stars did, small but distinct, sometimes unobserved, but always there in the night sky to lead the way, to remind people of a world whose horizons knew no bounds.

He sat on a bench and began his note, the tip of the lucky pen that Harriet had given him for his birthday caressing the paper in the same sure but gentle way he dreamed of caressing her.

"Dearest Heart," he wrote, then paused. In the distance, two elderly ladies walked arm in arm, their hats as feathered as if birds had dared to perch atop them. What advice might two older ladies have for him about how best to express himself to the one he loved? He almost stood, but thought better of it. They might be frightened by his sudden intensity. He did not think he could keep his voice calm, neutral, as he always did in the office. They passed by, bird-heads bobbing, and he wondered why ladies selected such hats, unless perhaps they had a secret wish to fly away. At night, birds nested and were not seen, just as the hats resided in their boxes. But what were all these thoughts, when his Harriet did not particularly like hats, and wore them only because it was expected? She wore no hat when she raced into the water, unless you might call a swimming cap a hat. Oh, she might wear a sun hat with a wide brim if she sat on the beach, but still he did not think she was the sort of girl who liked a hat, or who needed one to be beguiling. No, when he closed his eyes, he saw her in the black bathing suit with her neck stretched high, her eyes squinting in the sunlight under no hat brim, only her curly hair, slightly reddish blond, sheltering her from the sun's rays and falling to her shoulders. In the future, he thought, there might not be so many hats. Hadn't

bathing suits at first had long skirts that had become shorter and shorter until now they were cropped into short pants that hugged the torso? Perhaps hats would also become smaller, no more than a gesture, like a comma. But he was lost again in speculation, putting off writing the letter the same way he delayed writing his book.

"Dearest Heart," he began again, but this time his attention drifted to a figure in the distance, coming nearer. It was his friend Bill, the brother of his beloved Harriet, and he suddenly realized Bill would be accompanying them, and his heart deflated. He had envisioned just the two of them on the bench, two stars alone in the night sky who would each take strength from the other's burning bright.

Except that Bill was alone, and he veered to the right and took another path, striding purposefully in his blue suit, which became smaller and smaller until it seemed to meld into the sky. Lost in thought, Bill had just happened to be walking through the same park where Harriet had promised to meet Richard at half past noon. Bill disappeared, and some part of Richard felt ashamed that he had not greeted him. Earlier, he had thought of jumping up to greet two old ladies he didn't even know, yet he had failed to call out to one of his dearest friends. Was this what it was to be in love? Preoccupied and jittery and thinking thoughts as jumbled as the tails of ribbons?

He looked at the flower on the bench, alarmed as if the swaddled flower, like a newborn baby, was a miraculous new being whose name he had forgotten. Probably she would know and say its name caressingly, just as she would speak his. He felt his heart skip a beat as he imagined her saying his name. He had already written the greeting. Though he wrote, *"Dear,"* he envisioned her as a deer, bashful until twilight, daring to reveal itself in order to find sustenance as light faded. *Dearest Heart,* he wrote. He continued: *From the first days I knew you, you were destined to be a great lady—you have always had that extra something which takes people out of the mediocre class. And now, dear heart, I want to work with you towards the destiny you are bound to fulfill.* He looked at the handwriting and admired the penmanship. It was almost as if he held a magic wand, the words had flowed so smoothly. There was no going back, no redoing the note, though he wondered if the second salutation of her as "dear heart" had been merely repetitive, making the greeting less emphatic. It was the only piece of stationery he'd taken. He dared not make a mistake. *As I have told you many times*— He stopped. That was wrong. He seemed to be hectoring her, she whom he intended to treat so gently, as if she, herself, were swaddled in wrapping paper. How to turn that aside? By including himself, of course, by assuming they were already together. He reread and continued, anticipating the dash that would add a note of quickness and brightness to the letter: *As I have told you many times—living together will make us both grow—and by reason of it we shall realize our dreams. You are a great inspiration to me, and though you don't believe it yet, I someday shall return some of the benefit you have conferred upon me.*

It is our job (no going back, but a bad choice of words, as if the quotidian were tantamount!) . . . *It is our job to go forth together and accomplish great ends and we shall do it too.*

And, Dear One, through the years, whatever happens I shall always be with you—loving you more every hour and attempting to let you feel that love in your heart and life.

He blew gently on the ink, with so faint an exhale it might have been the stars' own breath expelled. Such notes were not written every day! Had he said what he meant, with enough conviction that it would be persuasive, providing scaffolding for their climb to heaven?

Another figure approached, a sudden parade of familiar people! Good heavens, was everyone going to be in the park at this important moment? It was Belinda Hayes, but she did not see him any more than Bill had, her eyes cast down with an expression of infinite sadness. Her cheeks were invisible, her hair almost obscuring her face. She looked at the ground, rushing on in a way that made him suspect she must be crying.

He was so lost in thought, he did not see Harriet coming toward him on another path. He missed her approach, missed the opportunity to gather his thoughts, lost any last chance to decide that the letter he'd tucked so carefully in its envelope was inadequate and must be rewritten, presented later.

"You seem lost in thought," she said, made melancholy by his own unexpected mood.

He stood awkwardly, fumbled for the flower, no doubt crushing some blossoms in his haste. The letter had fallen to the ground. This moment was happening too fast, yet was too slow to keep pace with his rapidly beating heart.

"I've missed you all summer long," he said.

"And written me a letter to prove it's true?" she asked coyly.

Her name was on the envelope. *Harriet,* written on the diagonal, as if the handwriting, itself, might lift off into space.

"You know," she said, smiling dejectedly, as if their greeting had been only perfunctory, "this is the park where Belinda Hayes and I last saw poor Gilbert Middlemark, who died. We were just little girls, and she kissed him on the cheek because he was so handsome, and he lifted her to a bench and said what pretty apple-red cheeks she had. They fancied each other, though she was much too young to marry, and the next week he was in the hospital, he had the flu of 1919, and he never did come home. She comes to the park because she's never forgotten him."

"Belinda Hayes?" He frowned.

"Why, yes," she said. "Do you know her?"

"She works at my office," he said immediately. "She walked by just a moment ago, and she looked so sad, but when I said good-bye and left the office, she seemed to be fine."

"If you're in love with her, you have no chance," Harriet said suddenly. "She says it's written in the stars that one day she and Gilbert will be reunited, and until then she will belong to no one else."

He saw, in Harriet's eyes, a sadness that transcended her years. Might she, too, have an unrequited love? And if so, was there any chance that he might be fortunate enough to be the one she loved?

"Bill told me she often comes walking in the park," Harriet said quietly. "Bill came to find her and try to lead her away from her sadness. He's your best friend. You must know his feelings about Belinda."

"But I don't," he said, for his thoughts had all been about his love, his yearning.

"How surprised you are," she said, "as if the park belonged only to you! As if you were here to see things, but no one could see you. Isn't that what a child thinks, hiding under the covers? If they hide, then Mama and DaDa can't see them?"

"Do you mean you and Bill have often talked about Belinda, and that he's known that I work with her every day, yet he never told me?"

From whatever harsh realities might he have been excluded? Harriet was looking at the flower, but he could tell that she was lost in sad thoughts, and she did not half see it. It could have been a pebble on the path, for all the interest she took. She was filled with compassion for both of them, for those who had already loved and lost something because of the intensity of that emotion, and in that moment he suspected that he might not know her at all, that her regret might be greater than that of Belinda, and her brother Bill. It was as if their sadness was her own.

"I wasn't so surprised to run into him," she said. "He knew where I was going today, because he overheard our call last night. And since he knows where he can often find the one he loves, there were two reasons to come to the park today, you see. When DaDa died, Bill made a solemn promise to look after me."

"Why would he think he had to look after you, when you would be with his best friend?" he asked.

Her eyebrow arched, telling him she knew more than she was saying. Though she, herself, would never write a book, she read the pages of his own heart. She was just waiting for him to catch up with what she already knew, as women so often waited tolerantly for men.

He was about to reach for her hand, its skin the lovely white of moonbeams, and raise it delicately to his lips, when she said, still lost in thought about other would-be lovers, "I think sometimes it makes him so sad, he only sees her from afar and goes away. I think he hopes the next time will be different."

A little breeze suddenly began to blow, and each watched as the envelope moved some distance in front of them. The things he did not know, lost in his dreams! Belinda, who was so young and helpful in the office—to think that she was waiting for her life to end, so she could be reunited with her lost love. Bill was one of his best friends, it was because of Bill that he had come to know Harriet, but men did not often talk to men about secret loves. He had never until now known Bill's secret. It came as a surprise to him that people could think things would change, that their life might change without even making a proclamation, without the power of their pen writing the most important words of their life. He took her hand, which she wordlessly extended, and its slight pressure kept him in place when the next breeze blew.

"Excuse me, does this letter belong to you?" said an elderly gentleman, strolling by, the tip of his cane planted on top of the envelope.

"Yes, I think it does," she said, rising and going toward him, her hair blowing backward, her skirt billowing around her slender hips, her hand outstretched. "Thank you very much," she said, delicately accepting the envelope with its delicate phrasing contained within, taking what she was handed ever so politely. He could only hope that, when she read it, she would say the same to the writer.

The story, written in the manner of F. Scott Fitzgerald, is fiction. The letter from Richard Nixon to his future wife is included as written.

Mrs. Nixon Reads "The Young Nixon" in Life, *November 6, 1970*

A beautiful winter day. A crow on the White House lawn, more birds in the trees. Sparrows, I think. Is there birdseed? Poor little creatures might need it, the ground's so hard. This morning the branches were encased in ice. Now it's sunny and wet and looks like a swell day, so of course my feathered friends are out pecking around. A great day for a walk, and maybe I'll take one after responding to some letters and glancing at the magazines.

Just back from discussing dinner with the chef: beef, with one of the red Bordeaux Dick likes so much. Tea for me. Prince Philip's dinner was a success, as were the midterm election returns. There's some possibility Mamie may join us. I hope Julie can be made to understand the importance of continued Secret Service protection. Spoke to Bob Haldeman and Bob Taylor of Secret Service about her desire to be left alone. I hope they will come up with some compromise. It is so difficult to always be watched. I know that! On my own, so young, no one to give any advice most of the time, because of work, work, work. Now, I could whisper over my shoulder and three people would come running. I wanted to ask Prince

Philip if it's true the Queen carries an empty handbag because she has no need of anything. I'm sure there's a Royal Handkerchief Carrier. It goes too far, really. The Prince has to walk several paces behind his own wife; I have to struggle to keep up with Dick most of the time, he walks so fast.

What a photograph of young Dick in *Life*: violin nestled under his chin, hair combed straight back, fourteen years old. Real musical talent, playing both violin and piano. Music is a thing that transports you. I must suggest to Julie that she listen to more music. That would be a way to "escape."

Someone has written to me, asking what to do about living in a building where there's never enough heat. I know just who to pass that along to, to get some action. Another letter had a poem written by an eighth grader on a typewriter whose keys were hit so hard they punctured the paper. Hey: that would make her the same age as Dick, on the cover of *Life*. You wonder how many people have talent that isn't recognized right away. Or how many fritter it away. How unusual to have periods at the ends of the stanzas, when lovely poetry usually drifts into whiteness . . . a poem about me, as a "treasure." Well, that's pretty nice!

(*Mrs. Nixon lights a cigarette, waves out the match. The burnt match rests on the rim of the ashtray.*)

Wonderful information about Dick and his many talents. A mention of the play he appeared in based on the *Aeneid,* and the information that Ola Florence Welch acted opposite Dick. Well, I didn't know him back then, so I've got no business being a bit jealous. She's always telling the press that he was so conservative, while she was always a Democrat—implying she's more enlightened. Well, bully! She looks like one of those F. Scott Fitzgerald flappers to me, one of those girls with not a bit of fluff to her hair, like she's wearing a big waxed mustache on top of her head. No wonder he was attracted to that mane of hair I used to have. Now it's cared for every week by my gal at Elizabeth Arden. Long hair isn't appropriate once you're past a certain age, but neatness always is. Ola likes to get her name in the papers. She's reminisced about things longer than the time they spent together.

Look at that photograph of Frank and Hannah Nixon. Always the same old one. The boys so blond, so well dressed. Poor little Harold died, and then Arthur, though he'd not been born when the photograph was taken. What's the expression? Not even a gleam in his father's eye? You know, Frank and the oldest, Harold, seem to be looking at a different person than Hannah and Dick and baby Donald. It's almost like two different pictures: the father and Harold in their dark suits in one, Hannah in her pale dress and her younger children in their white clothes in the other. Part of the family might have been watching the photographer, and the rest of them watching a cow or something. Everyone so serious and unsmiling. I guess it wouldn't have been appropriate to be grinning. A photograph was expensive, and nothing to laugh about. I'd know Dick anywhere, because of those level eyes. To think he was once a little blond boy, standing at his mother's side.

A pretty balanced article. Very informative about Dick's early years. So many friends are mentioned. Now, there are really only a few. Bebe, and Bob Abplanalp, Murray Chotiner. Become famous, and you leave so many people behind. Even if you're not famous, you do. Friends are for your youth, not so much for your adult years. Though without Helene, I'd die.

(*Mrs. Nixon flips through the magazine, settles on Letters to the Editors.*)

I missed the magazine with the piece Clare Luce wrote on that Ibsen play. Look how excited she got one reader! "Sirs: I was just about to scrub the bathroom floor when I noticed Clare

Boothe Luce's article, '*A Doll's House,* 1970' (Oct. 16). I became so engrossed I decided the floor and all the other chores could wait—maybe forever. Viva la Luce!—Anastasia Kelly, Forest Hills, N.Y." She probably still has to scrub her floor, but she wants her moment in the limelight, claiming to be a women's libber. Who'd name their child Anastasia, after what happened in Russia? I wouldn't name my daughter Emma, after Madame Bovary. Or Zelda, after that poor woman who went crazy. Anastasia! You wonder what they're thinking of.

And another letter: "Sirs: So Nora is leaving Thaw to find fulfillment as a woman—the new cop-out for the over-30 set. In my short-lived career (before marriage), I had important 'work of the world' to do, I dined at elegant restaurants daily. It is an empty world. Give me a peanut butter sandwich with my kids any day.—Patricia Gallagher, Fremont, Calif." Well, I do agree, but why can't both things be important, work and children? What "important work of the world" do you think our Miss Gallagher did? Was she a lawyer? A banker? She wasn't a pioneering photographer like that talented gal who's really made it in a man's world, Berenice Abbott, that's for sure! I don't see why it has to be a choice between peanut butter sandwiches, which I never made, or fine dining. You can make a lovely meal in your home, for very little money, and please the children, too. If you're a mother, that's what you're supposed to think about. I still do, though I'm lucky to have so much of the deciding delegated to someone else these days. What if I said, "Either I'm a mother or I'm the wife of the President of the United States"? Would someone insist I choose? Patricia Gallagher might realize it's not always easy to have what some would consider a privileged position. I'm happy for her that she thinks she's made the right decision, though. Better that than being in an endless quandary. So many people remain indecisive. There are those who see Dick as being a bit that way, but I see it differently. He weighs the pros and cons because he's responsible, not because he can't make a decision. He has such important matters to think about. In a way, everyone on Earth has important things to think about, but more of the weight of the world rests on Dick's shoulders. He's thinking for a lot of people—for the good of a lot of people—not just about what he thinks is best. I'm glad he doesn't strut around like Bob Haldeman, who's never in doubt about anything. I'd hate to be married to a man like that. I don't envy Mrs. Haldeman. He's fiercely loyal to Dick, and I approve of that, but he tries to intimidate people, and I don't have any respect for such behavior. You can always take a few moments to explain something, if you're so sure you're right. What if I acted that way toward Julie? She's young, but she's got a good head on her shoulders, and by golly, she married young, but right from the first, she was more sure than I was that she'd found the one for her in David Eisenhower. My Julie's a girl with pluck, and I admire a bit of pluck. Take any advantage you have and make the best of it, I say. Of course, I wouldn't want to seem to be cheering her on too much, as though she needed a pep team! She's smart and kind, and she'll do just fine, even if she might be annoyed at those Secret Service fellows doing their job, following her everywhere. Why, sometimes with Dick, in the early days, it was like he *was* the Secret Service, following me—or wanting to—everywhere I went.

(*Lights second cigarette from the package of Larks.*)

And here's a man with a lot of spunk. "Sirs: After reading 'A Doll's House, 1970' I feel for the first time that I understand what all those Women's Lib types have been getting at. Yes indeed. For a woman, Clare is a real fine writer." Well, she *is* a "real fine writer," and I know you're being witty, mister, but you know, maybe it's time to stop kidding around and listen. The same way the Nixons wanted to have a dignified photograph for posterity, maybe letter writing is wrong when it's dashed off instead of thought about carefully. You have to listen to that other voice inside your head that asks you a question, or that makes you feel uneasy, as if what you're saying might not be true.

I'll have to read Clare Luce's piece. I already think I'll like it. It might make me envious of whatever actress gets to play the wife's role in that play. Whether you agree or disagree with the character, one thing's for sure: if you're chosen, you throw yourself into the part, and you *act*. It's not about who you are, it's about who the character is. You have to get inside that character and believe in her, and if you can't do that, then you'll never be an actress.

All letters quoted were published in *Life*.

Serving Mrs. Nixon First

When Mr. and Mrs. Nixon were in the White House, usher (no kidding, usher) Rex Scouten (real name) was informed by RN that new rules must apply to the way things were being done. "If it is a mixed dinner, with a guest of honor, the wife of the guest of honor will be served first simultaneously with Mrs. Nixon, and then the guest of honor and I will be served second."

Nice that the ladies were served first, but did it give them any advantage as to when they could actually dig in?

Letters and Lies

In *The Time of Illusion,* Jonathan Schell makes a concise and chilling observation that allows us to see how Richard Nixon used fiction for manipulation: "The President had set in motion an elaborate hidden machine for manufacturing the appearance of public enthusiasm for himself. He had begun by making a direct appeal for support in the traditional manner. Then he had sent himself rigged telegrams and letters of support. Then he had put the telegrams and letters on display before the public that had supposedly sent them. Then he had arranged to have the Vice-President praise him effusively. Then he had apparently had telegrams and letters sent to television networks and the press praising the Vice-President for praising him. He had become his own most ardent and prolific supporter."

Was Mrs. Nixon aware of this? When the young Mickey Rooney exclaimed to Judy Garland that they could put on their own show (which of course the viewer has the ability to *overhear*), we smiled. But this was grown-up, behind-the-scenes nefarious-ness that had to be conducted secretly in order to work. He was a one-man band, but of course he also got to write the music, the reviews, then the positive letters to the editor about the reviews, and then go onstage again. Sometimes he thought it best to write a few negative letters, either to gain sympathy or to bring on more angry "supporters."

Ted Agnew, our Vice President until being forced to resign due to accepting bribes, was a mean sumbitch. He conceived of himself as a showman of alliteration and accusatory epithets and was generally regarded as a hothead whose main mission was to defend the President with whatever verbal ammunition it took. "RN" (as he conceived of himself) created situations and then found people to respond to the situations, then found people to respond to the people who responded, and so on. RN might have written some letters or telegrams himself—certainly he made notes, or voiced his opinions in meetings—but there were people hired to create these pseudodocuments who were bright and who had no doubt about what was expected. They made up a letter, ostensibly written by JFK, ordering the murder of President Diem. It has been suggested that E. Howard Hunt may have had a hand in the diary that was discovered in Arthur Bremer's apartment—in fact, the rumor was that Hunt might have both written it and planted it in the apartment: the "story" of his shooting Alabama governor George Wallace. All around RN, people were writing fiction whose purpose was to shine a mirror on a radiant President—radiant in his ideas, ideals, and leadership—and dazzle the public with the bits of light thrown off. He would have been too programmatic to be a good fiction writer, because fiction can't be hermetically sealed, but the genres RN selected worked well: a letter could be heartfelt and brief, a telegram more so. Few people automatically assume a printed letter is bogus—though RN inadvertently led the way to raising our consciousness about that.

In this age of cheap irony, I suspect people still credit honesty, perhaps even the much derided "sincerity." Healthy people can envision a sliding scale from total, soul-bearing honesty to sociopathic lying, and act somewhere on this spectrum. Their personal letters—those times they write them at all—can be explicit about the writers' real feelings, or as ingenuous as they think the situation requires, as insidious as they dare make them: they are works of fiction aimed at accomplishing what the letter writers want. Yet many recipients of letters assume they are reading something genuine; something that—for all the time the writer had to consider the prose—clearly means what it says, like graffiti. A letter can be more eloquent than the person's ability to speak such sentiments, or more awkward, but letter writing, as a genre, is associated with sincerity. The writer might aim for clarity, formal elegance, private confidence, but he or she asks to be taken seriously, to be read with care.

My friend Harry Mathews tells a hilarious story about how he came to meet Marie Chaix, his French wife. She had written a book that he'd been sent to consider translating. He looked at the gorgeous author's photograph, read the book, and knew he was in love with the writer. He wrote a letter, agreeing to translate the book into English, but realized, on rereading, that what he'd really done was write a letter that made clear he was in love with her. This wouldn't do; he wrote another letter, very much toned down, relying on all the advantageous forms of the French language to create more distance. This letter he sent. She received it and understood immediately that Harry was in love with her. So yes, you can reveal what you mean to conceal, even with much time to reconsider, or the letter can say one thing though the recipient will still read between the lines, or perhaps think that, though the letter is emphatic, actually the opposite information is implied. A letter does not necessarily protect its writer. A letter is a fabrication, a letter is the perfect vehicle for fiction (as RN knew, with some of the letters his staff wrote), yet in most cases, I think the letter's recipient does not open a letter and suspect a ruse. It's easy to understand why writers love to play with letters, real and invented: they seem to be private contemplations meant only for the recipients, so we (or the characters) have the impression we are confronted by the senders' innermost thoughts. As readers, we're always snooping a little when we read mail not intended for us.

When RN wrote his girlfriend Pat, he wouldn't have been thinking about the letter later appearing in her biography—but what a wonder it is, with prose so sincere it seems cringingly insincere, full of self-importance and feigned authority and speaking to an embarrassingly idealized future. Some letters do go public, and while their appearance gives us glimpses of the private person, it's really no guarantee that what we read is entirely genuine. Maybe we romanticize letters, wanting them to express sentiments that come closer to private truths, though experience requires we realize the mixed motivations that can go into writing a letter. Like reporting on dreams, letters dropped into fiction can appear too perfect, too contrived, as explanations or as ways of sneaking in additional information. Yet as documents that reveal more than they say, they can also convey information that reveals things of which the letter writer is unconscious: When F. Scott Fitzgerald writes about Ring Lardner's being discouraged by book sales and Fitzgerald asks Maxwell Perkins, "*Why* won't he write about Great Neck, a sort of Oddysee of man . . ." he asserts his best thought, though he reveals more of himself than he realizes. Writers have always loved to invent letters; they seem to be found documents and, as such, give the illusion of being out of the writers' control. They are so useful, they can seem so plaintive, they are set apart, they can explain things that would otherwise have to be elaborated in narrative. Surely, in a letter, we hear a person's "real" voice.

Richardson's *Pamela, or Virtue Rewarded,* considered by most critics to be the first novel, is epistolary. The plot—the abduction of young Pamela, who resists being compromised by her abductor, Mr. B—makes logical the format; Pamela, missing her parents, and wanting to let them know what a good girl she still is, is writing home. When her letters are intercepted, she instead keeps a journal. Finally, Mr. B does the right thing and proposes marriage, but what the reader thinks has been heard has been a sort of transcription of the young girl's life in the present—the ongoing "present" of the story. Though it was written with the intention of showing that virtue is rewarded, it's interesting that the author, in each subsequent edition of the very popular novel, relied on "readers' groups" for guidance about how he could improve the text, and ended up toning down the extremes: at first, Pamela's speech is filled with expressions of the lower class, but in subsequent editions, it becomes less conspicuous, so that the gap between her social class and that of her upper-class abductor, Mr. B, is lessened. The reduced linguistic discrepancy reassured readers that the two characters were meant for each other.

My story (ahem) "Desire" is about a young boy whose parents are divorced. He's visiting his father, and near the end of the story the father, B.B., intercepts a letter the boy has written:

> When I'm B.B.'s age I can be with you allways.
> We can live in a house like the Vt. house only not in Vt. no sno.
> We can get married and have a dog.

While understanding that almost everything is wrong with his son, B.B. addresses the immediate problem: the recipient is his son's stepsister, so they can never marry. Things deteriorate from the moment he explains. In writing the letter, I felt that I was taking dictation; I *was* the son, in the moment of composition. If he could speak to me, rather than just engage in dialogue with his father, this was what he would confess. I'd known his thoughts in general, but not in particular. Next, I gave thanks for the italics, which set the letter apart and focused attention on it immediately, as italicizing (though in this case I used old-fashioned underlining, to indicate italics on a typewriter). If it's in italics, it's important: not a mechanical contrivance suggesting distance, but right there, like something dashed off in real time. When I imagined myself as Bryce, the boy, the misspellings were automatic. (I particularly like "no sno." It rhymes, and the two words say a lot more than that there won't be any snow.) I hope the reader freezes just as B.B. does, that I manage to unite the reader with both characters, and to implicate the reader, too. It's obvious that, as mature readers, we are B.B. rather than the boy—obvious until this moment, when we see both sides of the problem simultaneously, but have no better alternative to offer than B.B. does. The letter seems indelible. It can't be undone, it will never be unread (we've read it), it will never be repeated. The writer (ahem) depends on the wow factor, though the letter is usual in its unusualness. It's the stopped time that's such a help, because it comes almost at story's end. The reader has to feel some small physical jolt. Also, the reader has to feel a little guilty—the value of ambient guilt can't be underestimated in putting together stories—because the reader has received secret information. You don't read other people's mail. And you certainly shouldn't read other people's mail while looking over their shoulders. In stories, though, if a letter is presented, you must open it and read. (My husband, before he was my husband, once mailed me a letter in an envelope that I looked at with dread, so sure of the contents that, instead of opening it, I drove from Virginia to New York to hand it back to him. Things worked out.)

Clearly, Mr. Nixon was not writing lovely, graceful notes to his wife, and later to his daughters, with any idea of producing something that could be used by a fiction writer—but imagine, for a moment, someone familiar with the life and times of RN (from our informed, present-day perspective), trying to reconcile the ardent letter writer with the man on the tapes, who is harsh, profane, racist, anti-Semitic. Were the lovely letters simply from an earlier period, and he changed? He was once the determined, clever suitor, then the proud groom. Were these occasions that brought out the best in him, rather than eliciting his hatred and contempt for his real or imagined enemies? Did he present one face that was benign, when the situation warranted that, and another that was vile, taping himself in the Oval Office uttering the verbal equivalent of strip poker? *Dr. Jekyll and Mr. Hyde* jumps to mind, but it's a bit extreme, and too expedient to be really convincing—and also, it's *literary*. If we knew such a person—certainly most of us know much milder versions—how would we reconcile our information? With some dismissive *Whew, some people are really nuts,* or by inventing some explanation, such as that he was under a spell, or that he was clever enough to put a lid on certain things to accomplish what he wanted, but that his real personality emerged under pressure?

Having read so much about Nixon in researching his wife, I came to internalize his voice, perhaps even his thought patterns—though I can't say where they originated for him. Where did his way of thinking and speaking come from—experience? The arrogance of power? Was this the same person who had an interest in theater, who enjoyed musical evenings at the White House?

Might he have been—I'm not kidding here—fearful? Intimidated, and therefore intimidating? Those curses and chilling dismissals of entire ethnic groups have the shocking effect of being deeply held beliefs, but what if he was using them as a crude way of expressing and retaining control or power, of keeping some primal fear at bay? If his affection was not involved, might he have existed on a short spectrum that stretched only from affability to paranoia and spitefulness because one extreme was nice but the other effective?

Henry Kissinger, who believed him to be anti-Semitic, did not confront Nixon with his thoughts, but muttered them to people who worked with him. RN's outspokenness was certainly a way to shut off discourse—to stun people into silence. People pay to swim in the presence of dolphins, hoping to absorb their reputed mammalian wisdom. Could we imagine the dolphins being called out to save RN from drowning in his malice? Imagine H. R. Haldeman suggesting, "Mr. President, when you go to Florida this weekend, you might want to try swimming with the dolphins." You can't; such dialogue is impossible. But wait: dolphins are supposed to be drawn to people who are ill. Not only is their touch said to be healing but they seem to have a sense of their potential usefulness. They seem to function in agreement with one another and to choose the problematic over the usual.

Writers are dolphins.

A Story Occasioned by Considering Richard Nixon and Dolphins

Richard Nixon, in his red, white, and blue bathing trunks, stood with Bebe Rebozo, his longtime confidant, at the top of the pool where the dolphins swam. He expected Bebe to back down—Bebe would understand Dick wanted him to be the first to back down—but Bebe seemed out of sync with him today, preoccupied, a bit dazzled by the motion in the water below. "Well, I hope those fellows down there know to vote Republican," the President deadpanned. Bebe Rebozo smiled. He found his friend the President a very amusing fellow. Look at that bathing suit! He, himself, was wearing his usual black swim trunks with a white stripe along each side, properly faded from being out on his boat, on the glistening water he loved. He put a hand on RN's shoulder and registered the fact that RN stiffened and stepped backward. There was a blond woman, mid-twenties, who'd been assigned to explain how things worked in the water, but the Secret Service were still talking to her, and the one agent who remained by the pool seemed as dazzled by the surface of the tank as he, Bebe, was. He would have to speak to the President about the people protecting him, but this did not seem to be the time. The agent bent and touched the water, staring at his fingers as if examining a dipstick. "Well, there's really not much time for this today, if we want to get in the boat," the President said. "We'll come back another time, and thank that yellow-haired mermaid who was going down in the tank with us for her trouble." He was speaking more to the agent than to Bebe Rebozo. "I have heard the mermaids singing, each to each, all of that," the President said. "If we can't eat those fellows, we should get some fishing poles and try to catch some fish we can eat."

Bebe Rebozo was not quick on the uptake, the President noticed. Also, Bebe did not read poetry.

"Mr. President?" the Secret Service agent said. He was wearing blue swim trunks. There were swimming fins on the ground beside him. A snorkeling mask.

"I bet they'd be surprised to see us stick up a bank in these getups!" the President said, "but maybe today we'll just go fishing."

He waved the agent away—why did they so often simply say, "Mr. President?" as if every time he saw them, he had something to say? He walked toward the door, where another agent stood guard. If the guard said, "Mr. President?" as he approached, he was going to ask him to jump in the tank to test the water temperature. That would be a good one. Quite the story to take back to the others.

But the agent stared straight ahead—all right, it was an odd assignment, but he was the President, damn it—and Bebe Rebozo suddenly turned, ran to the tank, squeezed his nostrils shut, and jumped in. That was good: the President didn't know how to dive, either. Fine to just jump in. Bubbles rose to the surface. In there without any mask, he'd be up in a minute. The President gave the Secret Service agent a smile, raising his hands to indicate: boys will be boys. He had used the same gesture often, on television, it had been pointed out to him, when he was emphasizing a point. The less hand action on TV the better was the bottom line. Viewers were made nervous by hands moving around. His hands hung at his sides, waiting for Bebe to surface. He suddenly remembered that there was one more adjustment, or—what would you call it?—another transfer that Bebe Rebozo had to make by shifting some funds so that he could buy Pat diamond earrings for their anniversary. Good of Bebe to do it, but that was Bebe: loyal. He'd stood as stiff as the groom atop a cake during his wedding to Pat, and what a cake that had been, with real flowers on top. The room in the hotel had been rented—the Presidential Suite, whose name turned out to be productive (wait a minute: *prophetic* was the right word), and then they had taken a road trip for their honeymoon, which began as soon as their allotted time in the room was up. Which made him think: Where the hell was Bebe? Was he pulling one of his practical jokes? Well, he would just wait and see. Outlast them. That was the ticket: outlast 'em all.

He'd done the right thing in finding Pat, finessed the outcome by being patient. He was a man who could be patient. He was being patient now. Bebe down there with the fish, and some half-assed Secret Service man drowning with him, well, that was the price you paid in the job, and there wasn't a job you could get without paying a price. Let any of those Secret Service fellows go on television and tell the whole world how much he made, how much he spent on gold cross necklaces for his Catholic girlfriend, from the looks of it, him with his Irish face, he'd be Catholic, and so would the girlfriend, and they could say, Thanks, Pope, and breed into eternity.

Next agent into the pool, and where was the other one, who'd disappeared with the mermaid? Probably having quite a time with her, wiggling their tails. Well, that was understandable. Dress yourself in that kind of bathing suit, you're asking for trouble. Of course, you can't always get involved in giving people what they want, because they ask for one thing, then, once they've got you involved, it can turn out they want another. Then another and another, and so on, until you can't give them any more and you have to get rid of them.

There was another agent replacing the one who'd torn off his shirt and jumped in the tank . . . this was getting funny. Something to tell Haldeman about, show him how his plan turned out: Bebe dead, all the Secret Service fellows dead, a whole tank of drowned people, well, what could you expect, a harebrained plan like that? Good to have free enterprise, but a dolphin tank was going too far, better that people do an honest day's work. Or send 'em to Hanoi. Let the intellectuals figure their way out of that.

Everyone was expendable. Let 'em drown in a tank of sharks, that's what they deserved, on their way to audition for another goddamn rainbow poster with its Commie hippie peace and love propaganda that numbed young folks like another one of their drugs, and kept them from becoming contributing members of society. Mrs. Nixon would agree that a good day was a day that involved hard work, and so would the girls. They'd married young but completed their studies, that was the right thing to do, and Tricia even read and liked *The Rise and Fall of the Third Reich*.

He went to the rim of the tank and shook his fist at the water until the bubbles disappeared. Oh, in some storybook you could find magic and whatnot, but in real life there were known dangers and unknown dangers, and this one hadn't made a fool of Nixon. Let the impulsive ones jump in and drown, and those who went after them, all in the pursuit of what? Pleasure. Well, now they saw what happened.

The presidential helicopter would lift him out of this sorry place, and he'd look down on all of it from the distance from which it deserved to be seen: high in the air, as high as the pilot could fly— and of course someone would have checked the pilot's credentials, and so forth, making sure he was a good Republican.

My Anticipated Mail

Dear Ms. Beattie,

You reveal yourself to be a smug fact bender. Why don't you leave President Nixon to history? If you're writing scurrilous things it must be fashionable right now because what have you ever done that's original? History will decree that he is a different person than the one you present so simplistically, but I suspect you are looking for book sales, not truth.

Dear Anne Beattie,

Your book seems to slander a man who has been criticized enough. You obviously do not know the real Mrs. Nixon. I notice that your thoughts on her were not printed in *The New Yorker*.

Hi, Professor Beattie!

I was in your short story class in 2005 when we read the Frederick Barthelme story about doing that dance step you got up and showed us, saying you felt old because we'd never heard of it. I have continued to read Mr. Barthelme's stories.

I would like to know if you could write a letter of recommendation for me for a Fulbright. You can download the instructions directly from the website. I have attached the link. In case you don't remember me, I'm enclosing a picture of me taken with Professor Blair (printed in *UVA Magazine*), who suggested I take your course. My sister just finished reading *Janus* in high school. Vanessa Prince (she has a different last name from me) also may be coming to U.Va. I'm telling her to take your class!

In advance, thank you, Professor Beattie. I know many people must make requests on your time.

Dear Mrs. Beattie:

As a fighter pilot in the Air Force, I led several strikes against Rabaul in New Britain. We flew P-39s out of Bougainville and refueled at Green Island coming and going. We were also there on D-Day. How much we appreciated Lt. Nixon's hamburger stand on Green! As rushed as we were, I would never leave without those refreshments.

It meant so much—just a few minutes' relaxation, good sandwiches, and the coldest pineapple juice in the islands. I didn't know then who our benefactor was. I'd like to thank him now on behalf of the 347th Fighter Group.

The final letter is real, and was written by Chandler P. Worley of Indianola, Mississippi. It was sent to *Life*, where it was published as a letter to the editor. The real salutation is "Sirs."

Merely Players

Mrs. Nixon thought about being in the movies, as many attractive young women living in California did, and still do. The first Mrs. Reagan was in the movies. So was Mrs. Nixon, but her tiny part in *Becky Sharp*, a lackluster 1935 movie based on Thackeray's *Vanity Fair*, was cut. You can understand what she'd like about being an actress: acting was something like travel—moving into another identity; moving to another place—and Mrs. Nixon's love of travel was part and parcel with her love of freedom. Even going away to visit her aunt who was a nun seemed to her like freedom. Julie Nixon Eisenhower reports that her mother liked the glamorous costumes an actress got to wear, though she did not like waiting around while the director did retakes. Standing around a movie set wouldn't appeal to most people, but you can imagine that Mrs. Nixon found it frustrating in part because it was a demystification of the art of moviemaking. If she ever thought the people involved in the process were in some way special, that illusion disappeared when one of the directors of *Becky Sharp*, who fancied her, got drunk and went to her apartment and carried on. Her brothers were there, so that was that. Still: not exactly a magic moment.

How much did Mrs. Nixon know, years later, about her husband's attempts at fictionalization? He'd been an actor, too, briefly.
But he went on to write his own scripts, so to speak. Others enacted
them, but he was like a movie director on a national scale. He
even tried his hand at costume design, putting the White House
guards in outfits out of a Marx Brothers comedy. RN was also the
scriptwriter (old joke in Hollywood: "She was so stupid, she slept
with the writer"). During his administration, a telegram was pho-
nied up to give the impression President Kennedy had ordered the
assassination of President Ngo Dinh Diem. In *The Time of Illusion*,
Jonathan Schell writes: "By the spring of 1972, President Nixon
was setting himself up as the scriptwriter of the whole of American political life. He looked upon America as his predecessors in
the White House had looked upon Vietnam: as a great theatre
for a sweeping dramatic production, in which a real nation was
used as the stage, real public figures were used as unwilling actors,
and the history of the nation was used as the plot." He was actor,
producer, director, screenwriter, costume designer, outdoing Orson
Welles. More protesters, more pesky extras than had been called
for, mobs of them, showed up on the set, but he hoped to mitigate
their power by instigating a campaign of letter writing sympa-
thetic to the President. It was so extensive that publications and
television stations assumed it must be a real reaction. This was a
bit like flashing the "applause" sign for the studio audience. The
audience, of course, was his own staff and those to whom they
delegated the task of mass mailings. Nothing suggests Mrs. Nixon
knew about this at the time, though if she later came to read about
it and believed what she read—what *could* Mrs. Nixon believe?—
she must have been quite surprised. She was a patriot. She was a
loyal wife who believed her husband was acting for the good of
the country, but "acting" had connotations she would have been

shocked to consider. No matter: she'd become just a member of the audience, along with everyone else.

The marginalized person's point of view is always informative, as is that of the unsophisticated person, who perceives with limited awareness (Faulkner's child narrator), or that of the minor character. Tom Stoppard's *Rosencrantz and Guildenstern Are Dead* was a big hit: the two men who accompany Hamlet on his voyage—their POV, instead of the main character's. (Also John Gardner's *Grendel*; Jean Rhys's *Wide Sargasso Sea*.) It's a common problem that can turn into an advantage, when a writer creates a minor character who won't stay in his limited role and insists on dominating the scene. Sometimes this can be the voice of the Sirens, trying to throw the writer off course, but more often it's an indication of some sort of shift within the material that is causing it to escape the writer's grasp. Stoppard didn't stumble into writing a play about the two messengers, but many writers will tell you that in revising, to their surprise, they realized who the real subject of the piece was—whose story it was. And if the writer sticks with the original plan, it's nonetheless possible that another writer will come along and sort out the initial story differently, so that characters on the periphery of the action are recycled and re-presented, with different emphasis, through a different writer's sensibility.

For me, Mrs. Nixon became a minor character who would not keep quiet. She was so often silent (the Checkers speech; her final exit from the White House) that it's tempting to think she had little to say. Writers tend to love people who volunteer very little, for their silence frees the writers to project onto them, though such characters are also confusing. Why are they so quiet? We now know Mrs. Nixon was too pained, leaving the White House, to speak; that she was given no lines to say in the highly orchestrated Checkers speech. But was she acting? It seems likely that she was, during the Checkers speech (she felt the accusations against them were unfair and didn't want to make a response), though it was a different matter, and she was just trying to keep it together, as she said her good-byes to the White House staff. Acting shouldn't be thought of negatively; everything could be known from her gestures, from her silently grasping the staff's hands. But a penny for her thoughts, years earlier, as she sat ramrod-straight in a chair while her husband explained their finances to the nation, on TV, and his insistence upon keeping their gift dog. Those thoughts could have been pretty much anything, but if they appeared in fiction, the reader would, justifiably, have certain expectations that had to be met. Interpolating with a unique approach (perhaps Mrs. Nixon was thinking: I should be a Buddhist) would seem to suggest that the writer was obtuse, or worse, that the writer was revealing something about himself/herself but nothing, really, about Mrs. Nixon, who would have to have the thoughts *anybody* might have in the moment.

Yet how can writers be sure about what *anybody* might think? Especially when writers think as little as possible about *anybody* and almost constantly about *the exception*? Err in the direction of giving an account of that generalized "anybody" and Mrs. Nixon's interior life would be so predictable, it would be as unconvincing as it would be boring. More interesting would be to imagine something within the realm of Mrs. Nixon's imagination. A role she acted in, for example. Maybe *Becky Sharp*. Contrast her role in that with her presence as a minor character in the Checkers speech. It would also be credible because both moments were public performances, though diametrically opposed, for in *Becky Sharp* the title character is rebellious, flirtatious, manipulative, and gets away with wild misbehavior.

Mrs. Nixon is a fictional character only to the extent we all are, having both public and private selves. Journalism may be more effective than fiction in offering a new perspective on a public figure because when facts are informative or telling, they automatically redefine. A list of ten things we wouldn't expect of Mrs. Nixon immediately tells us that she isn't a stereotype (for example: Mrs. Nixon knew how to change a tire). How to come up with a fictional equivalent—to surprise and inform us about Mrs. Nixon without merely being facile and fabricating? (To be avoided: Mrs. Nixon's dreams, a conventional easy shot.) Since the public persona is what we can see, albeit distantly, we have to import such information into her private sphere. Onstage, Mrs. Nixon stood where she was told to stand and delivered her lines, but the writer follows her backstage to her makeup table, where she daubs at her greasepaint, looking intently in the mirror, surrounded by a mandorla marquee of lights. That is where the fiction writer—like any other member of an admiring audience—wants to follow, or intrude.

Mrs. Nixon Lies, and Plays Hostess

The news of President Eisenhower's heart attack on September 24, 1955, sent camera crews and reporters to the Nixon home. Vice President RN was there—shocked by the news, but at home—though a plan was quickly concocted to have Bill Rogers, Acting Attorney General, spirit him away, so that he would not have to come up with reassurances. Eisenhower's heart attack is one of RN's "six crises": crises in his life and how he triumphed, basically. If one could generalize, one could say that any "crisis" was a red flag and that RN was a bull. There was no "running away." However, if he could spend the night elsewhere and temporarily evade the questions, that was acceptable. He writes: "As I hung up the receiver, I suddenly realized that Pat was unaware of what had happened and I went upstairs and told her the news. I then telephoned my secretary, Rose Mary Woods, who was still at the wedding reception, and asked her to go to her apartment so that she could handle the incoming telephone calls on an extension of my house phone located there. Pat in the meantime had tried to break the news, as quietly as possible, to the children."

My interest here is not merely in the narrative ("Pat in the meantime"), but in giving the reader a sense of how people reacted, what it felt like on a scale of 1 to 10 for both Mr. and Mrs. Nixon to hear that the President was out of commission. Certainly we can believe that Mrs. Nixon was composed, but her husband's tendency to rush the narrative gives the reader no breathing room in which to form any assessment of people's real states—the thing I'm most interested in. It would have been uncharacteristic of RN to digress into Mrs. Nixon's response, to her real emotional state, because he saw only the important integers in a story (Nixon and Eisenhower). He never stopped to consider anyone but the primary players.

So: Mrs. Nixon got the news about President Eisenhower and probably said, what? "Oh, Dick!" and immediately ran off to the rooms of her two daughters? Even if she did, the fiction writer would be alert to a general awareness of mortality, of conventional dialogue that would have to be presented truthfully (truthful to the character), but, since it would indicate almost nothing, and could seem to be a conventional contrivance of the writer, and therefore a liability, something else would have to be offered immediately, so that this would be not a generic story about a traumatic moment but something that revealed to the reader *these* people in *this* traumatic moment.

In the chapter called "The Heart Attack" in *Six Crises,* RN hurries to get to the point. To instruct us. He feels that the essential narrative has very little, if anything, to do with how people *felt*. He would not have noticed, and therefore would not report, whether Mrs. Nixon might have stumbled on her way to see Julie and Tricia, or whether the family pet perked up its ears. No, what mattered was that, because something was happening to the President, something was happening to RN. This is the narcissism of mediocre storytelling. The narrator is going to provide us with only the important players in sharp focus and let us assume what we want about extraneous figures, like Mrs. Nixon. (It is interesting that one of the daughters gets quoted, blurting out: "The President isn't going to die, is he, Daddy?" while Mrs. Nixon is only wordlessly animated.)

More things happen: the Acting Attorney General, summoned, arrives at the Nixon home—and, in a skit from a comedy routine, Mrs. Rogers, waiting on a side street in their Pontiac for her husband to leave the house, finds that both her husband and RN jump into the car, having left by the back door when one of RN's daughters inadvertently got the attention of the newsmen outside by going to investigate, so the reporters didn't see RN or the Attorney General quickly cutting across the neighbors' lawn to the waiting car.

Did RN say good-bye to his wife? (Not reported.) They had arrived in Bethesda in approximately fifteen minutes, we learn, and his hosts for the night gave Mr. Nixon a pair of pajamas, a toothbrush, and a bed to sleep in. Did RN call Mrs. Nixon? He does not say he made a call to her. He says he slept badly—in fact, not at all—but there is some glee in having escaped the press.

Mrs. Nixon, however, is stuck with them. Maybe she isn't if she doesn't open the door, but their job is to show up and wait, and Mrs. Nixon is herself, so at some point she has them in and offers refreshments downstairs—not in the main house, but in the finished downstairs. Previously, she has lied to them, telling them that her husband was not home, that she does not know when he can be expected, and—offering a bit of good advice—telling them they'd do better to call his office in order to keep posted.

As a fiction writer, I want to know: What do the daughters do when RN disappears? Does Mrs. Nixon have an easy time reassuring them, or is it difficult? At what moment does Mrs. Nixon decide to be nice, and to have the members of the press in (even though it's only to the basement) and serve them something? Is she on autopilot, or does she sense something that makes this a more genuine gesture? What is it like for this woman to be with people it would be unwise to communicate with? Does a water bug scuttle across the floor? Has one of the bulbs in the overhead light fixture burned out?

A couple of days later, RN took his wife and daughters to church, where the minister prayed that the President's health be restored. RN then invited some reporters back to his house (living room), and, of course, RN was hardly spontaneous, if anyone might have mistaken his gesture: "My first meeting with the press, in which my words, my actions, even my mood, would be reported to the nation, for me was a crisis. I wanted to be prepared for it as best I could. Even my manner of my meeting the press, no matter what I said, could be subject to misinterpretation. . . . If I refused to see the press altogether, it might indicate a lack of confidence or even fear—and this would be a reflection upon the whole Administration." RN put on an act. He doesn't tell us he rehearsed his lines, but he does tell us he was guarded, fearful, intent on making a good impression. Where was Mrs. Nixon, even if she vanished into the house, into the background? Did she try to overhear, or did she go upstairs, braid her daughter's hair, hem some clothes . . . What did she do? A minor character doesn't disappear just because the major character loses sight of her. Does the phone ring unexpectedly? If so, should we assume she answers? Is anything served to the guests? The Nixons don't have servants. It would boggle the mind to assume RN might do the serving.

Of course an essay about oneself is going to be self-serving. (*Six Crises* was written pre–memoir craze, in which self-bashing became almost as much fun as complaining about everybody else.) If you are an animate version of the Sun, there is no reason that you should constantly look toward Pluto and Mercury. But for those of us who know there is a solar system, exactly how at ease are we going to be if planets or galaxies or stars we know are there simply flicker out? How much are we going to trust an inadequately narrated story?

Many do trust journalism, though recent problems with Pulitzers having to be returned from *The Washington Post* and plagiarism at *The New York Times* and *The New Republic* have opened people's eyes. Readers of fiction—which is supposed to be artifice—have a somewhat easier time, because the narrator, when not taking the pose of being some transparent, hovering presence, is a character in the story—meaning, as potentially flawed as anyone under his or her consideration. The unreliable narrator is sometimes insistent about being a force in the story (André Gide), sometimes cleverly withholding, even in ostensibly making a confession (Ford Madox Ford), and sometimes simply someone so acclimated to warping the truth that the purpose is to puff out a fog of words, as the main character prevaricates.

Russell Banks and Peter Taylor have been interested in narrators who seem to reveal themselves but gradually present contradictions (Banks's "Sarah Cole: A Type of Love Story"), or who never reveal the cards held close to the vest, though the reader, as the story progresses, watches the vest disintegrate (Taylor's "The Old Forest"). In fiction, our tendency is to believe what the narrator tells us. We have no orientation to the story initially; we're at the mercy of the information given to us. Whether or not we are of the same class as the characters isn't a big issue—at least, not consciously. We are taught to trust voice. We are taught to listen to someone's tone (a bit angry? defensive?), as well as to the words spoken. Autistic people, who can't "read" tone, have a problem because of this lack of perception. Nuance, inflection, allusion . . . it doesn't exist in their awareness to inform them. A smile is a world apart from a grimace, but an autistic person does not perceive the difference. Fiction is all about covert winks, deliberate stumbles, things happening off the page, allusions that function as scaffolding. Metafiction announces, and inherently questions, itself.

In primary school we were taught to give earnest reports on, say, corn production in Kansas, and we came to believe in the reliable story. Like RN, we think we should stick to the facts. But what story unfolds without complexity? We are not supposed to digress ("I might be wrong here, but I think the light was red. . . .") because we are telling someone else what *happened*. But *why* are we telling the story? Why is such value placed on what happened? Maybe we're telling the story because we were in a fender bender, and we want sympathy. But even when we tell what we think of as a simple story, listeners form impressions the storyteller can't shake: X has always been a bad driver; X is gesturing wildly, a bit too defensively; X should have been at work when this happened and has not said why she wasn't. We'd go crazy if we did nothing but listen to subtext, read body language, and extrapolate meaning in terms of what we know about the person telling the story while simultaneously introspecting about our own desires, assumptions, and fears. But at least when the storyteller is present, and admits to telling a story, we can fleetingly experience these things as additional elements. We understand that at least two stories are happening simultaneously (theirs and ours). Fiction is no different, except that we have not a person in front of us, but rather that person's voice (which we make a mistake to conflate with the author's, even if we've met the writer). The disembodied voice is more difficult, and because writers know this, they usually work to create a character as well as a narrative voice, trying to make the character come into focus so that the character will seem physically as well as psychically recognizable, and therefore more convincing. If only voice is relied on (Beckett), we are startled.

Peter Taylor often adopts first-person narrators. There is a faux friendliness that can proceed for some time before the reader begins to suspect something is up. Many reviewers never understood what Taylor does, and still think that affable, Southern Peter Taylor was writing about affable, slightly loquacious, and slightly befuddled Southerners—*but aren't Southerners that way!* Perhaps they often are, so that, really, Peter Taylor set himself a very hard task: both to accurately invoke and to expose the narrator. To ask us to rely on our knowledge of geography, terrain that we may not have seen, and how it was "back then," though many of his readers never experienced it—the unmistakable smell of apple pies baking that Grandma never made for us, though we *believe* in Grandma's apple pie. It's sacred. It's our American myth. It's unreal.

RN was not exactly an unreliable narrator. He believed he could tell a story for his convenience and still persuade. If he's telling the story of General Eisenhower's coronary, then it is about the General, and it is about RN, the General's Vice President. Leave it to the ladies' magazines to sweep up and let us know Mamie Eisenhower's three rules for functioning in times of stress. (A hypothetical example, but I'll play my own game: make fudge; talk to your mother on the phone; put on your fur coat to feel warm and safe.) If RN's nonfiction account of this "crisis" had been fiction, Mrs. Nixon's dropping in and out would have looked like it was orchestrated by an inexperienced writer who assumed that, at the writer's whim, a character could disappear and conveniently reappear.

I think that RN put his wife in his account because he was reporting truthfully (to his way of thinking) what happened.

Because he never sees (or acknowledges) her as a real force, though, he lets her get away because she probably *did* drift away. She was used to doing that. My inclination would be to track her, though: upstairs, into her bedroom, into the bathroom, wherever one had to go to find her. If everything is really as RN says, then the way she puts on her nightgown would affirm his insight, her whispered assurances to her daughters would contain no ironies (intentional or unintentional), we—along with the writer—could risk including her at the conclusion. But all we have is a mention of her at a dinner given by Alice Roosevelt Longworth, and then her husband continues *his* story, in which General Eisenhower had numerous health problems, but he, RN, has passed through this "crisis" and learned a lesson he wants us to understand, as well. As usual, it has something to do with not being a coward, with facing things down, with acting. In the last paragraph, he grandly widens his scope so that we understand: "They were to a less and different extent personal crises for me. But even more, they were potential constitutional crises of the greatest magnitude for the nation."

Oh. And upstairs, does Mrs. Nixon fumble and slip into her nightgown with a sigh? Does she go to Julie's bedroom and peek in and wonder if Julie might be pretending to be asleep to spare her tired mother from having to say something else consoling? And because sleep has something in common with death, does Mrs. Nixon think back to her mother's illness, when she sat at her side through the night as her mother lay dying at the home of the doctor who diagnosed her illness? Does she recall sitting, later, at the bedsides of TB patients, and who knows (though anyone could guess) what happened to them?

The fiction writer in me wants to know: who let the dog out?

Prophetic Moments

Princess Diana's sisters, upon learning of her reservations about marrying Prince Charles: "Too late, Duch, your face is on the tea towels."

Mrs. Nixon's best friend, Helene Drown, upon learning that Eisenhower had chosen Nixon as his running mate: "Oh, Pat, you're going to be in the history books!"

My Meeting with Mrs. Nixon

Yes, I met her. There was a store in downtown Washington called Woodward & Lothrop ("Woodies"), where my mother often took me shopping. My mother always got more pleasure from dressing her daughter than from dressing herself—with the exception of high heels. One pair for her, one for me.

I wasn't a Birkenstock sort of girl. I wore high heels to college.

I met Mrs. Nixon not in the White House, but in the shoe department of Woodies. Tricia was with her, but at no time did she say anything. She looked pleasant but unapproachable, while Mrs. Nixon seemed almost giggly. Several Secret Service agents were in the area. Perhaps more I couldn't see.

Mrs. Nixon was trying on shoes. If Tricia didn't need shoes, or if nothing appealed to her, I don't know. But many shoes appealed to Mrs. Nixon. Some had a higher heel than I'd seen her wear in photographs. One pair had an ankle strap, but she didn't even close the strap—just slid her foot in and out, talking to her daughter about something I couldn't hear.

"Do you belong with that group?" my mother said to me. It was the same comment she made to my father, those times he stared in restaurants and listened too intently to another table's conversation.

Every salesperson in the area was pretending not to notice the Nixons. Mrs. Nixon sat with her coat folded on a chair next to her and shopping bags on top of it. Her daughter sat on the other side, with her coat on the chair next to her. The coats and packages were blockades, in case anyone wanted to plop down and visit. My mother was not even sneaking looks; she feigned interest in a mannequin being dressed in the lingerie department.

A Secret Service agent looked at me, blank-faced; I dropped my eyes and leaned a bit toward my mother. I was twenty-two years old, back in Washington on vacation from graduate school in Connecticut. It was 1969. In a bag at my feet was a long nightgown (Connecticut was *really* cold in those days) and some other small purchases, I think. But the shoes were what I was really interested in, impractical as they were. They had a very high heel and were a burnt orange color with black ribbons twined across the front. The toes were neither round nor pointy. I remember these shoes so distinctly because my mother bought them for me. It would have been counterproductive to tell my mother that I wore several pairs of kneesocks under fishing boots to walk the pathways of the snowy campus. The beautiful heels could be an art object. Come spring, I could wear them.

The Vietnam war was going on and on and on. That totally left my mind, that day. There seemed no larger context than Mrs. Nixon and Tricia and their coats and bags and . . . the fact that she was trying on the same shoes I was! These were not Mrs. Nixon shoes. They were not. She'd topple exiting an airplane. And they wouldn't be comfortable to stand in a receiving line. Dancing? She'd have to be pretty adept.

"No?" she said, turning her foot sideways.

She was speaking to me. And I was sitting there with the same shoes on both feet, not standing to try them out because I was so mesmerized by her.

"We wore these in the forties, didn't we?" she said to my mother.

Indeed my mother had. Every picture of my mother showed her in such shoes. This color, though, was new. My mother's shoes had been black or brown, or white, in the springtime.

I *felt* it, the bond between the two women.

"You get them because they're beautiful shoes," Mrs. Nixon said to me.

This doubled my chances: though they were expensive, both my mother and Mrs. Nixon admired them.

A Secret Service agent picked up Tricia's bag. Tricia looked at him briefly, wondering if he was hinting that they should leave. He stood there with the bag. Then Mrs. Nixon noticed what Tricia was noticing while at the same time noticing that we, too, looked at him, puzzled. And then all four of us smiled, understanding that this was a man who'd had enough of shopping. He just wanted to go.

"I'll get you those," my mother said decisively, reaching for her wallet.

"I'm going to be the customer they hate to have, who can't find anything that's exactly right," Mrs. Nixon said.

But no one hated Mrs. Nixon. Not me, as someone who hated her husband's politics; not the blasé salesladies who would talk about it for days to come; not my mother, who had established a little blip of recognition based not on who she and Mrs. Nixon were in 1969, but on their having been young women who had bought high heels and worn them to work during the Second World War.

Woodies is gone. My shoes are gone (how could that be?). When we left, my mother said: "I raised you well, not to do something silly, like ask for an autograph."

I Didn't Meet Her

But you wanted me to have met her, didn't you? Because books are always about the author, however well or badly hidden, as well as being about the book's subject. Writing just *isn't* impersonal. My story brought me forward, for a moment. Even if my little story wasn't very momentous—or maybe because it wasn't—it seemed *real*. It was a clue about the author and the author's project, but now has turned out to be a lie. So the work of fitting together the author, her subject, and how to understand the text is suddenly thrown back to the reader. You certainly won't fall into *that* trap again.

Readers have a desire to know the author. They can read biographies. If the author is hip enough, they can read the review and look at the author's photo in *People*. They can look at pictures of "Literary Lions" in evening wear at the New York Public Library in *New York* magazine. I do. I study those pictures. I study them because they're all I have of the person behind the text.

If I'd met her, it would at least partially explain why I was writing about Mrs. Nixon. The reader could understand the spark—though just a little spark, granted—that must have ignited something in the writer's brain.

I didn't meet her—no more fooling around, nothing follows to contradict this—but I did shop with my mother at Woodies during the time Mrs. Nixon was First Lady. As a fiction writer, I did an okay job of bringing in the Secret Service—a detail you'd expect, with just a little something erratic added. I loved those shoes and can't imagine where they went because I certainly never wore them out, and they would be as stylish now as they were then.

My mother got old and wore sensible lace-up shoes that ladies her age wear. I have a ridiculously large shoe wardrobe—a way, perhaps, to resist moving into old age; one friend recently wore her super-high-heeled Etro ankle straps to my door, carrying another pair of shoes in her purse. She knew I'd squeal in admiration, and—since they didn't fit her comfortably (or she was kind enough to say they didn't)—she was there to hear my squeal and to step out of them and generously give them to me. They fit perfectly, and are the prettiest shoes I own.

But how much do you want to hear about me and shoes? Even if shoes are a way of talking about something else?

Is what you've been reading fiction or nonfiction? Or is it my memoir, which appears—like certain weeds, I can't resist saying—only in the cracks? Years ago, in the seventies, a journalist who later became a friend had just become editor of a magazine and was receiving manuscripts that were subtitled "A True Story." Then it turned out they were—by the author's admission—fiction. Similarly, he received stories in which he recognized real people, barely disguised. That, however, he could grant was fiction. But about the others . . . the ones that identified themselves as being true when they were not: how was he to understand, exactly, what was going on? "Ann, what is fiction?" he said, striking terror into my heart. When he asked, I thought he wanted me to get into some philosophical discussion. "You can ask them, if you're confused," I said, lamely. But didn't I wonder whether they would tell the truth? Oprah once believed in "emotional truth," until there was something of an uproar and she changed her stance.

While I was working on this book, I was sent the 2008 Pushcart Prize anthology: the best from the small magazines. In it was a poem: "Skinny-Dipping with Pat Nixon," by David Kirby. I almost jumped out of the chair. Someone else, thinking about Mrs. Nixon! (I am quoting only part of the poem.)

But now I'm the age you are in the portrait, and I can see
how hard it was for you, how different it would have been
if you'd had a good marriage, a good man.
I would get in that pool with you, Pat; as the guests swirl, unseeing,
you'd turn your back to me and wriggle out of

your old-fashioned white undies, dive in and surface
where I wait, then throw your arms around my neck.
I brush your hair out of your eyes and glance down
at your breasts, though I'm too shy to touch them.

The poem made me smile a big, nervous smile. Someone appropriating Mrs. Nixon, but the poet addressing himself to her, directly! It's a complicated poem, but the Browningesque direct address increases the intimacy (which is also, in part, the poem's subject). The poet is right, I think: as we get older, we realize the price people pay for posing for the portrait, in effect. Writers might also feel that sometimes they can rescue the moment, even rescue the past. So many times, that's the case—that necessary delusion that allows writers to write in the only time period they have, the present, but with the flexibility and with the audacity to look forward as well as backward. Writers see the irony of Gatsby's famous line about recapturing the past—it is what he believes, or needs to believe (interchangeable), but it is not factually true. Only a pedant would stop at this point in *The Great Gatsby* and note that the character's observation is untrue, however. It's more important that it informs us of his delusion.

"Skinny-Dipping with Pat Nixon" is not exactly analogous, as the author certainly knows he addresses a dead person, but he seems more determined in his intent on resurrecting her (her, rather than himself). Whereas Gatsby wants *his* Daisy, his interpretation of Daisy for his own sake, not to empathetically release her into being the version of herself she wants to be. Also funny, Kirby's poem is a serious matter about where the laughter starts and ends, as we learn more shocking things from biographies all the time than that a person not likely to run naked into the water went skinny-dipping.

RN, ousted from office, wanted to recast himself as an "elder statesman." Mrs. Nixon . . . for all we know, she wanted to go skinny-dipping. For all I know, she would have liked those shoes and nudged my mother in the direction of buying them for me. We can say what's predictable, based on what we know of a person's life, but as writers we also have to deal with the unforeseeable. Writers, as well as readers, perk up when some such thing is discovered. Or even when it is invented, if the invention seems possible.

Flannery O'Connor, writing about science fiction, says that the writer has to write so that "even when one writes a fantasy, reality is the proper basis of it. A thing is fantastic because it is so real, so real that it is fantastic."

The Writer's Feet Beneath the Curtain

Fiction writers rely on dialogue to carry more meaning than the words themselves convey. We're used to people saying one thing and meaning another, and we're used to people blurting out something unexpected: verbal flares of anger; secrets suddenly spilled. Dialogue takes advantage of those moments, but if the writer relies too much on things happening suddenly, the reader is likely to become skeptical. A character's impulsiveness can seem to be a convenience for the writer rather than a convincing character trait.

Dialogue can be useful when it gives off enough energy to allow us to read around and through the words, offering us a way to know the characters as we interpret them, not as the writer insists we view them. Dialogue seems to happen in real time: *now,* the characters are talking. The writer's narration, however, happens in literary time: the writer has sorted things out and presents them with the coherence of a story being told, instead of with the unfolding immediacy of dialogue. The freshness of dialogue is, of course, an illusion; the writer comes up with whatever is said and can revise. But as characters speak, their dialogue has the effect of making us suspend literary time and pay close attention, as if we're getting someone's real thoughts in real time, as they occur.

Dialogue can be useful to the writer simply because it interrupts exposition that has gone on too long—the way a sneeze can break up the monotony of a long conversation. People create their verbal contexts as they move from one environment to another. A cell phone conversation will use different language, and take a different form, than what is said by the person who walks into a meeting to make a presentation, though in most cases we adopt language much more conventionally than we like to think. Fluent cliché lets us belong, but we prefer not to think of ourselves as formulaic clones. People can come up with their own language and, once they learn it, rely on the words and expressions they feel comfortable with—which means that their speech becomes predictable: the person's daughter is "The Princess," his car is "My Beamer." Mr. Nixon's wife was "Mrs. Nixon." The writer has to create enough recognizable speech to be convincing, but also to particularize the character by using words or phrases unique to that person. In the same way we're startled in real life when someone steps out of character (at least when he or she varies conventional roles: the polite waiter; the brave soldier), we are surprised, in fiction, when a character plays against type. But writers couldn't write if characters didn't do this. There are wonderful works of fiction in which the character does not change, but instead goes through the motions of a life. Even then, the writer usually steps out to dazzle at the last possible moment, offering a lyrical passage at story's end that superimposes the writer's more expansive sensibility, the writer's potential to dazzle, previously withheld to better reveal the character's limitations. (It's not a value judgment; some people are more guarded, inexpressive, or creatures of habit than others.)

An example would be Edward Loomis's "A Kansas Girl," in which a woman lives an unremarkable life with her father, never marrying, doing her job until she eventually retires, then takes a trip to the Grand Canyon. Hers is the frightening cliché of what life might be—all that life might amount to—that motivates many to live differently. A fear of serving in this way was at the back of Mrs. Nixon's mind long before she became Mrs. Nixon. Loomis writes about his character, at the Grand Canyon: "She left by train in the last week of July (calm, slow, a little vague), bound for Los Angeles and San Francisco, and her first stop was at the south rim of the Grand Canyon, where she found the buildings pleasant and recognizable. She stayed at the old hotel, a high shingled structure that could have had a respectable place in Kansas City; she went to the rim and was astonished, and she noticed many other people her age along the sturdy rail." Because we believe in the limitations—or at least the repressed nature—of the character, a description such as "she went to the rim and was astonished" does not seem like lazy writing, but is a narrative voice imitating the way the character, herself, might modestly recount her own story, speaking in restrained language.

The narrator, to this point, has been in collusion with the main character, though the narrator will eventually step away from her at the end of the story. Then, sentences—the writer's sentences; language the writer has held in check, providing a few hints but giving the illusion of merely reporting, going along with the limitations of his character—appear: "She stayed two days, and felt happy; and her trip was a success—on her return to Kansas City she was ready to die, and seven years later she accomplished this end: her mind was pure, and once, in the hospital, she thought of her father, remembering as a child how she had been able to call him to her, where she lay pale and cool in the narrow bed—a good father, who would be coming toward her out of the glistening throng." Wow. All the writer's restraint has been in service of this moment, which expresses his empathy with his character, what was always his ability to see the character in a completely different context, his awareness of her imagination, whether or not she imagines things in the same terms as he. He becomes her spokesperson. Then he eclipses her. He's watched life creep along in its petty pace until the moment he decides to ignite the engines and achieve liftoff, shooting straight for the stars.

George Garrett, in "An Evening Performance," focuses on an event as lavish as Loomis's story is rooted in the quotidian. The performance (circus acts) described in the story is extraordinary, but instead of ending on an even higher note, Garrett quotes "a wise man" (always suspect, in contemporary fiction). It is, of course, the author orchestrating this final moment, making us uncomfortable with our assumptions. "A wise man said [the performance] had been a terrible thing. 'It made us all sophisticated,' he said. 'We can't be pleased by any ordinary marvels anymore—tightrope walkers, fire-eaters, pretty girls being fired out of cannons. It's going to take a regular apocalypse to make us raise our eyebrows again." Notice the pairing of *regular* with *apocalypse,* which parallels the combination of *ordinary* with *marvels.* The author appropriates a folksy tone, pairing words that might be skipped over because they seem to be spoken in the vernacular. They are a big clue to the reader, though, because they are disjunctive. Then, having simultaneously called up and dismissed the "wise man," Garrett steps in a second time, to give us his—the narrator's—even wiser opinion (though not advertised as such): "He was almost right, as nearly correct as a man could hope to be. How could he even imagine that more than one aging, loveless woman slept better ever after, smiled as she dreamed herself gloriously descending for all the world to see from a topless tower into a lake of flame?" *Almost; nearly; could hope to be* . . . the words seem to sympathize with the plight of the average person, while really that person is exactly the one the writer wants to leave behind in the dust. Garrett is the prophet who knows that other people wouldn't know unless he told them. He focuses on the exception, the extraordinary, the way something has the potential to change one person, profoundly. At story's end, the author gives a highly valued gift: imagination. That's the liberating force, both in Loomis and in Garrett: the card game played expressionlessly until the ace is finally revealed. Such stories go to extremes (the blandness of everyday life versus the extravaganza of a circus act) to seem to narrate something familiar, already understood. Each has the resonance of a morality tale, and some of the suspense of fairy tales. But both genres are invoked only to be turned aside. The author prevails, possessing the power of the imagination as the key to escape. There's a strong authorial presence, even if it's not obvious—*because* it's not obvious—until the last moments of the game.

The writer has remained hidden in both stories, taking care that his feet aren't seen beneath the curtain until he chooses to walk out—but in Loomis's and Garrett's stories the writer *does,* finally, choose to appear. In more contemporary stories, the author usually doesn't display a last-minute, radically different sensibility, but remains offstage, so that we can only infer things about the writer through the trajectory of the story and because of the shifting language chosen to tell it. One reason any story goes on as long as it does is to condition the reader to its milieu, as distinct from what the reader might rush to *assume* the world of the story is. The writer as spokesman—ironic, or tongue-in-cheek master of ceremonies, or last-minute lyrical poet—has pretty much disappeared from contemporary stories, and dialogue is relied on not so much to show communication between characters as to reveal the lack of it. When dialogue ends a story, it often asks or implies a question—one that becomes cosmic because of its placement, and would make the respondent look foolish however the person answered. The killer last line of Salinger's "Uncle Wiggly in Connecticut" speaks to the story's subtext; any answer offered would be unsatisfying. To ask the question makes it obvious that no answer would make anything any different. The point of the question is that it is unanswerable.

Within stories, though, dialogue must seem neither contrived by the author to impart information nor chitchat to convince the reader that the characters are real people who, of course, talk. When they speak, it's the reader's way of taking their pulse. Consider Mrs. Nixon, and what she is reported to have said from her wheelchair, leaving the hospital after her stroke: "But the stress of Watergate and the illness of her husband took their toll on Pat. On July 7, 1974, she suffered a stroke that crippled her left side. Two weeks later, wearing a yellow pants suit and a bright smile, she left the hospital in a wheelchair pushed by her husband. 'I feel fine,' she beamed with a nod toward her husband. 'But I'm a little frightened about the driver.'" It's a characteristic attempt at being amusing, and at deflecting attention from herself. If RN makes a response, it isn't recorded by author Elizabeth Simpson Smith. It's the sort of remark that requires no response. Also, why not let the person in the wheelchair get the last laugh? As his wife's straight man, his role is easy to play: just a big smile. Her comment is the verbal equivalent of a wink: *You and I know* . . . A woman who did not like to talk publicly, she managed yet again to get away with a one-liner. What about fear (his and hers)? The fiction writer would have little interest in her quip, but be fascinated by what was or wasn't said inside the car.

In "Why I Write," Joan Didion describes her writing process:

When I talk about pictures in my mind, I am talking, quite specifically, about images that shimmer around the edges. There used to be an illustration in every elementary psychology book showing a cat drawn by a patient in varying stages of schizophrenia. This cat had a shimmer around it. You could see the molecular structure breaking down at the very edges of the cat: the cat became the background and the background the cat, everything interacting, exchanging ions. People on hallucinogens describe the same perception of objects. I'm not a schizophrenic, nor do I take hallucinogens, but certain images do shimmer for me. Look hard enough, and you can't miss the shimmer. It's there. You can't think too much about these pictures that shimmer. You just lie low and let them develop. You stay quiet. You don't talk to many people and you keep your nervous system from shorting out and you try to locate the cat in the shimmer, the grammar in the picture.

Taking a tip from Ms. Didion, I looked for a long time at the picture of Mr. Nixon wheeling his smiling wife toward their car. We don't have—you can be sure we don't have—the photograph of her as she got into the car. As for the two smiling people, that's uninteresting. When they could let those expressions go, what did her face look like? His? We don't have enough to interpret the emotional undercurrents of the moment. This image is the campaign poster, as opposed to the snapshot of the unposed politician. Their public faces, her supercilious talk . . . to have heard the first words spoken in the car would have been a revelation, but his taping system was in the White House, so we have no record of that exchange. Invented dialogue? "Dick, in case this happens a second time, I want you to know . . ." What would she want him to know? What would he say, if he began the conversation? "Pat, it's been a rotten time for you, but . . ." How much did she listen to him at this point? Both were suddenly in uncharted territory—traumatized, humbled, perhaps trying to appear, to each other, stronger than they felt. People tend to like being in control, or appearing to be in control. Good dialogue can express what a character wants (or, more to the point, what he might think he wants) while at the same time giving us a sense of how much distance there is between that desire and the way things are.

Here's an example of dialogue that seems to veer out of control as we listen. It's from "Duncan in China," by Gish Jen—a long story about a man with little awareness of how the world operates, who visits China and meets his ill, desperate cousin, who has hoped the visitor might be his (and his son's) way out of China—though he soon grimly realizes this will not happen. Guotai, the Chinese cousin, has brought along his son, Bing Bing. He gives the boy beer and encourages him to dance on the tabletop. "'*Good dancing, good dancing!*' cried Guotai. 'Show him what his Chinese cousins are! Embarrass him to death! He's here to visit China—show him what our country is. In China, you can dance, you can starve. Still people act as if they do not even see you! Show him! You watch.' Guotai turned to Duncan, his eyes glittering strangely. 'This is China! Nobody will say anything! You watch!'" The hysteria of exclamation points involves the reader in Guotai's frenzied excitement. We can *see* it. The dialogue informs and alarms us. The comma that intends to link things together emphatically is also almost deadly, itself: "In China, you can dance, you can starve." We're rushing toward something, and the idea of death is overt: not only has it been mentioned in a seemingly throwaway phrase ("Embarrass him to death!") but it becomes even more explicit when dancing and dying are yoked, as if there is inherent logic to their pairing.

In the same way we're all the characters in our dream, we're Guotai, Duncan, and Bing Bing: we're the perverse master of ceremonies; we're the awed and frightened audience; we're the helpless child who is performing, out of his mind. The moment will go on as long as it does because it and we are out of control. But the dialogue isn't: it does just what the writer intends it to do, operating explicitly and subtly—"embarrass him to death" may resonate, at first, only as a figure of speech. When the words have done their work, however, the writer concludes the scene with exposition: "But he was wrong. In fact, a hostess was already headed their way with a frown on her face when Bing Bing passed out and fell into the tureen of duck soup." Conjuring up the Marx Brothers (*Duck Soup*) is clever and underscores the seriousness of the situation: this isn't harmless slapstick, this is real desperation.

As a writer, what do you do either with dialogue that is badly written (unconvincing, for many reasons), or—always a possibility—when you have only the words of people who are not speaking genuinely, but as actors who've written their own unconvincing script? Monica Crowley's *Nixon in Winter* is a book about a young woman (Ms. Crowley) who works with former President Nixon during the time he is living in New Jersey, written from the point of view of an admirer. Mrs. Nixon—though she lived in the same house the author spent so much time in—figures in the book very little. However, there is a scene in which Mr. Nixon first introduces Ms. Crowley to his wife:

"I want you to come meet Mrs. Nixon," he said on July 12, 1990, shortly after I began working for him. "She's in the office today to do some things, and she knows you have joined the team,

and she'd like to meet you too." He walked with me from my office to the conference room, where the former first lady was seated, signing autographs for a charity event. "Pat?" he said. "This is Monica." She looked up, smiled warmly, and took my hand with both of hers. "Well, hello. I've heard so much about you. Dick tells me that you're right out of college. What a wonderful opportunity for you to be here." I thanked her, and she squeezed my hand. "Don't let Dick give you a hard time, now," she said, smiling at him. "If he does—well, just report it to me." He turned to me. "Are you going to squeal on me?" "Only if you give her a reason to," she said, winking at me, and Nixon leaned forward and gave her arm an affectionate squeeze.

There's no reason not to accept the words the author says were spoken, but except for their being too formulaic to be informative, almost nothing was communicated among the three people, who instead stuck to their lines. It's believable RN spoke of "the team." Mrs. Nixon's kindness is also recognizable as a polite verbal blockade. You yearn for someone to pound on the door and scream "Fire!" to see if anything would shake them up, make them drop their transparent but apparently exquisitely adequate defenses. Ms. Crowley has been presented with a common problem: no one gave her anything. She recorded the nothing she was given, but, in so doing, she gives us nothing as well. The problem with this account is that it seems inevitable in a way that is deadly dull. People are enacting a ritual, everyone aware of what's expected, everyone playing a role, while pretending their roles are unscripted. A fiction writer would have to do more than say Mrs. Nixon was signing autographs, would have to make us *see* something (her handwriting? the paper?). We can't see anything in the meet-and-greet scenario, though, because the focus is on the people, not the world they inhabit. The dialogue is banter, its intent to communicate that everything is going along according to plan, rather than that what is happening is precarious and relies on everyone's playing along. Nothing shimmers. As hard as the reader looks, there's nothing to see because nothing is particularized. As Ms. Crowley narrates the scene, everyone gets to occupy his or her own discrete space; in fiction, those times there is no physical motion (she, at her desk; he—never an expressive man, physically—standing stiffly), the writer has a vast repertoire of ways around this stock standoff. What did Ms. Crowley, as an outsider, see that Mr. Nixon and Mrs. Nixon did not? Presumably, nothing. Could we expect her to write, "But I wasn't about to take them at face value, so I asked whether they were aware that they were stonewalling"?

Predictable dialogue condescends to the reader and makes us yearn for what we hear between the lines; paradoxically, bad dialogue sharpens our sense of what really might be said, what *is* being said under the surface and off the page, at first indistinct but building to a crescendo so that finally we're happier sinking under the surface instead of floating at the top, stranded with characters who bore us.

King Timahoe, with a Coat
Neither Cloth nor Republican

(The Writer Fast-Forwards into Mrs. Nixon's Future)

M any dogs preceded him, and other dogs would follow, but King Timahoe was a special favorite of the President. Training a dog was of no interest, however. It was a dog. Dogs acted like dogs. The President was not under any illusions about dogs. They ran around and did whatever they did. Got into things, and all that. Sure to cause trouble. Animals: you'd expect them to present some problems. There was always somebody to take care of them. Put Alex on it. Have him talk to Manolo, if need be. Mrs. Sanchez. They had a bird, themselves. Well, they couldn't add to the problem by bringing in a dog, could they? They could, but it wouldn't be right. They had ideas about propriety and so forth. Those were the days, back in the White House.

Did Mrs. Nixon try to train any of the dogs, or did she secretly sympathize and take some satisfaction in their causing trouble? It's obvious that some people want to live vicariously and acquire pets so they can misbehave in ways the owners wouldn't dare.

One wonders if Mrs. Nixon did any vicarious living through Mr. Nixon. After her stroke, when she was not as able to cope with things, Mr. Nixon found a dog wandering on the property at their home in New Jersey and brought it home: their new pet, Brownie. She is reported to have found its behavior irritating. It survived her, though, and provided companionship for her husband, though he was happy to let other people feed it and walk it. (He would have preferred the companionship of whatever president was in office, but the phone calls seldom came. He disdained Carter and Mrs. Carter, whom he imitated, calling her husband "Jimmah." There was a *lot* of waiting for the phone to ring, as you find out if you read Monica Crowley's *Nixon in Winter*. President Clinton did call. Good for him, RN thought. He could impart quite a lot of good advice to Mr. Clinton.)

What exactly do you do if your husband brings home a dog? Checkers was a gift, as we all know, but in the case of Brownie, Mrs. Nixon was no longer even steady on her feet: Mr. Nixon found the dog wandering one night when he went out to take a walk, and then there it was, trotting in the front door.

"Oh, Dick, it must belong to somebody."

"Well, we don't know. It might belong to some people down the road, but we don't have their number. You know what I mean: we don't have their *telephone* number. Not the sort of number I keep on the Rolodex, it goes without saying. Fine to exchange a greeting, but what do you do with phone numbers except that they mount up, business cards, little pieces of paper. Before you know it, you've got the names of a lot of people who could be anybody, and why would you call them? We could let the dog wander. We could do that, but we don't know it wouldn't get into the road and find itself in trouble. Is it wrong to have the dog in the house this one night? Well, maybe it is, but it isn't right to let a dog go on its way when it might be killed. You look for a tag, or something. But nobody took the time to put a tag on the dog, and my point is, that tells you something. It could also be a dog dumped by some kids from the city, getting tired of it and driving it all the way out to the suburbs, just to get rid of it. They see these big houses, they think, Oh, they're a bunch of bleeding-heart liberals who'll take in a dog on a cold night. Some people do that, invite street people in, so some of them end up killed. Cold out there. I'm going to fix a cup of tea. Would you like some?"

"Let me do it."

"You remember that trip we took, all your shopping with Mrs. Gorbachev, and the way the press didn't want to talk about anything else? Damn fools. Why, you got the groceries all your life. Mrs. Gorbachev was told to go buy groceries that day, you can bet on that. If they'd told her to put on her bathing suit and take a swan dive from the highest spire on the Kremlin, she would have done that, too. Groceries! They didn't want her taking you shopping for expensive clothes and so forth, because there were none to be had. I suppose they could have airlifted some in from Paris. Had a fashion show for you ladies at the hotel. The Arabs do that to keep the women happy."

"Dick, I don't think this is the right time for us to have a dog."

"Is there a right time? I suppose it's always better when you're young. What isn't? Though maturity does have its advantages. Things get clearer. You take action because what are you going to do, sit around and wait for the grandchildren to pay a visit? They do, and it's good of them, but you know what I mean."

"Dick, if we feed the dog, it's going to want to stay."

"Dog's in the other room. Doesn't seem so interested in food, but we might give him a bowl of water."

"I'll use this bowl."

"We had some great times with the dogs, didn't we? Oh, everybody didn't understand. A dog's an expense, that's for sure. But you see the delight in your children's eyes, what should you do? Some parents would say No! Walk away. But we didn't do that."

"Tricia called this afternoon. She's going to come for a visit."

"Julie will come, too. Won't she?"

"I've only heard from Tricia, who's bringing Christopher."

"Boy likes to run around. A boy and his dog. Well, that can be *our* dog. Would be a good photo opportunity. Christmas card, and all that. Get the neighbors to come on over, crowd around and smile, give them a photograph of them with the President and his family, informal, something they can keep for posterity. I got a letter last week saying I was the most misunderstood president of the last fifty years. Where the fellow got our address, I don't know, but it was nice of him. Got to remember to make a note to have Monica write him back. Send him one of those bookmarks with the presidential seal."

"Dick, what do you think the dog is doing?"

"I guess I could ask him. It's a 'he,' I saw. He was peeing against our tree."

"Here's the bowl for—"

"Don't you bend over, I can do that. Is the heat on high under that teakettle? I don't notice it whistling."

"The whistling kettle rusted. We have to replace it. Julie said she had an extra one she'd bring us."

"I wonder if David will come with her. Kids will, but David might be working. I don't know what he really thought some of the time, when things were so bad and so forth, but he shows up a lot more than Eddie. Eddie said some things he shouldn't, but that's water over the dam. Been a fine husband and father. You hope they will be, but you don't know when they marry so young. Here's the bowl. Looks like a pretty good one. Of course, we wouldn't have bad ones. What would be the point? Some might say, Well, we never clear out our old bowls, chipped and dented and whatnot, but here in the Nixon household, Mrs. Nixon keeps watch over the bowls and replaces them when there's reason to. Of course, Mrs. Nixon is thrifty, which is a virtue not often valued enough these days. Glad to know Julie has an extra kettle. All the neatniks and recyclers and those sort would be happy, too. Keeping the landfill down. All those sorts of issues they think about. Drinking water. Well, if you boil water it's safe, but try telling that to some people. They have a big family, they don't have time to boil water. We boil water and we're doing our part as citizens, which we've always done, though at times we've been misunderstood."

"Here's your tea, Dick."

"Some might say the President has people who write all his speeches, tell him his own thoughts, but that wouldn't be right. I used so much pencil lead, I could have drawn a line down the Great Wall. Automatic signature thing was helpful, but there are those who wouldn't even notice, just want some indication they were heard. I can understand that. You express your thoughts, you want a response. You're not writing to Stalin, you're writing the President of the United States. In the old days, Rose Mary would send off an immediate response if I flagged something. She'd jump to it, just like the 'Star Spangled Banner' was being played and she was in the bleachers. She had special seating, of course, because she was part of the President's team. Took some criticism for it, too, but she understood politics. That's one of the things I respect. Loyalty. Remind me to speak to Monica about answering some of the mail. Piles up, otherwise. Not enough time to do everything. Other presidents understand. You know, the Johnsons never did have us to the White House, but the Nixons weren't petty that way. You know as well as anyone we weren't; we talked about those lists, and you stood in the receiving line how many times? Bet you didn't keep count, did you? You should have, because you deserve credit for standing there, shaking hands, no matter what. Lady Bird was always nice to you, but he was a different character. Spoke to me from his bed that time I visited the White House and never did get up. Then again, I'd heard he talked to people sitting on the toilet. Showed the nation his scar, where he had his gallbladder removed. Very involved in himself. Lady Bird wouldn't disagree. Her name was what? What did you call Lady Bird?"

"Lady Bird. Her name is Claudia Alta Taylor."

"Lady Bird's just as good."

Mr. Nixon took his tea into the living room, where the dog lay by the fire. The dog looked up.

"You're not having tea?" Mr. Nixon said.

"No. I think it's about time to turn in."

"Might watch some television? Not that I care, but if you do, let me know whether Clinton got himself in any trouble today."

"Dick, why don't you take the dog out and see if anyone is looking for it?"

"Brownie, here? Well, they might go looking, but unless they're invited to come in and sit by the fire and have a brandy—I'm only kidding—well, they could come in, and, if there's hot water, they could have a cup of tea, too, and we could be like those people in England, having a cuppa. Harmless. Or is it?"

Mrs. Nixon held the railing, walking upstairs. He wanted her to watch the news, but she was tired. The next day, she'd make some inquiries about who might own the dog. At least it had cheered him up a little.

She used Elizabeth Arden cosmetics, but washed her face with Ivory soap. It didn't lather too much—just the right amount. With some of the new soaps, she felt like one of the witches in *Macbeth*, urging the fire to burn and the cauldron to bubble. She realized that was a strange thing to leap to mind, when she was only going to wash her face. She did sometimes think of *Macbeth* and meant to reread it. She used no moisturizer. She brushed her teeth before going to bed, and again upon awakening. Her hair was always limp in cold weather and didn't have any bounce. She didn't know what to do about it, except put on a scarf.

The loneliness was like sea glass. It was attractive, sometimes. But it could also retain sharp edges. She had sometimes looked for sea glass on the beach in San Clemente, and Fina had cautioned her about picking it up because the edges could cut, even when the rest had been worn smooth.

Who knew that later the glass gathering would be good exercise, lifting little things out of the sand so her bad hand became accustomed to opening and closing normally. Bird feathers held no interest, shells rarely caught her attention . . . sometimes she still drew something in the sand with her toe, or sometimes she used a stick and made a quick drawing the water would wash away. That was back in California, of course. Their Elba. After they'd settled in, Fina and Manolo Sanchez went away. The loneliness was very much like sea glass, if sea glass could be a state of mind. Loneliness was always smooth. Activity had been worn down to smooth loneliness. Like sea glass, loneliness had a sheen. She could almost feel it, close her fingers around it, but she was exhausted, and there was no beach outside, so she only rested her hands on top of the covers. It weighed on you and exhausted you. The strokes contributed, but really the problem was loneliness.

Maybe they should keep the dog.

At Mr. Jefferson's University

"She's like writing about this wife of the President? She was famous for sitting in on some TV program about their dog that was some scandal or something? And I'm like, Oh. I am *so* not looking forward to seeing my dad this weekend, but I am chuffed to be in at This is br ing up. Oh, some book she's ing, she goes, 'I'm writing a boo about Mrs. Nix .' Like she isn't always ing so retarded."

Mamie Eisenhower Is Included in Tricia's Wedding Plans

Mamie called yesterday, and I think it might be a nice idea if we invited her to come over for your fitting, Dolly. It's fun for girls of whatever age to be included in these things. Oh, I already knew you'd say yes, but I wanted to make sure before phoning her. Mamie sounded a little down, so this should be a pick-me-up. She's always adored you girls. And also, there was a call to double-check the embroidery. It's to say: "Gown by Priscilla of Boston for the White House Wedding of Tricia Nixon to Edward Finch Cox (dash) June 12, 1971 (dash)." Is that right? Such a good idea, Priscilla had.

"Someday my own daughter might wear that dress, and it will mean so much more to both of us."

It will be your secret and hers that there's commemorative stitching inside the hem. I know you haven't decided on your shoes yet, but please do think about heel height and not go too high. Once you decide, you can wear shoes to the fitting that are the same height as the ones you'll wear at your wedding. I'm sure you and Priscilla will talk about shoes, but do be a little practical there, because you want to feel comfortable as well as pretty on your special day.

This afternoon while we're gone, someone from the staff wants to replace one of the crystals that dropped from the chandelier in your bedroom. I think they want to give it a good cleaning, too, but I told them that now wouldn't be the time. Many things can wait until after the Big Day. I've put the crystal in my desk drawer for safekeeping; they were so distressed to see it there, with the vacuum almost running over it, and who *does* know why a crystal would just suddenly drop? Now they want to inspect everything. I said, "Let me have it for safekeeping, and as soon as the wedding is over, you can bring in the ladder!"

I'm choosing "afternoon length" for my dress. It's spunky and fun, as well as being flattering. Priscilla will use white crepe and overlay it with organdy, covered by lace blossoms. Some will be pale blue, and here and there will be some yellow flowers. It will all be very subtle and fancy and feminine, which she has such a talent for creating. There are a few pink flowers, too, in among the blue and yellow. It sounds a little too bright, but it's really just beautiful—I've seen the fabric. I'm wearing my white T-strap heels.

"That will be pretty."

Quite a different wedding from the one your father and I had in California. We rented the Presidential Suite, though, so I guess we had some intuition! Priscilla is carrying the dress in a suitcase on the plane, so no one can see. She's so thoughtful and careful about whatever she does. The staff signs a confidentiality agreement so no word will leak out, and I do think that's a good precaution. I think I'll write her a little note, even though I thanked her on the phone. A note is something you can look at again. A thank-you on the phone is just like a cloud passing by. Conversations fly away!

The wedding presents are coming in all the time. You'd never get to your own wedding if you had to attend that many showers!

But wasn't Mamie cute, laughing out loud at you in your white feather boa?

"You're always saying that nothing's wrong with having a little fun."

And there *isn't*. She had such a good time that day. That is not the sort of thing a military wife would actually have, but I guess, if I had it to do over again, I could wear a boa like that twirled around my neck with my Republican cloth coat . . . though maybe that's all best forgotten. Every now and then I think about a few funny things I could do, and one of these days I'm going to surprise everyone and just act up a bit! I was so amused by seeing you in your yellow apron imprinted with the information: "Julia Child Eats TV Dinners." Well, she's a busy gal, so what if she does? I'm still recovering from Martha Mitchell's gift, but when you think about it, it does let you know Martha has some perspective on herself. A gold telephone! Her husband wouldn't have found it one bit funny. If he has any sense of humor, it's lost on me. If you have patience with Martha, you know, when she settles down she has interesting things to say. I'm fond of her, though sometimes she goes too far.

"You're a good friend to Mrs. Mitchell."

One of the staff had a cart he was using yesterday. Pushing the presents down the corridor with a shopping cart, and someone coming behind him with a handheld present that was apparently very delicate. That's the White House version of going to the market, I guess—though I never had anyone bringing up the rear when I went shopping. We'd be lucky to have something like that, wouldn't we? Back and forth all day with gifts, and more to come, they must be thinking. You are going to have many lovely things to begin your life with Eddie in New York.

"Yes, but I don't ever want to iron. You iron beautifully, but I've never learned to do it right."

Tomorrow morning Priscilla will be in the Diplomatic Reception Room, and what do you say Mamie and I have a cup of tea and let you talk to her alone for a few moments? She might have some questions she'd like to ask privately. I don't know *what*, just that she might. The designer and the bride might want to talk over some things that don't involve two older ladies. Well, I appreciate that. She'll be flying into National Airport, just the way she did for Luci Johnson. She's a real goodwill ambassador of beautiful bridal dresses, isn't she?

"She designs the most beautiful wedding dresses."

Last night your father asked many times if things are coming along all right, and I know he's very proud of you and excited about this important moment at the White House. He's worried he won't be good enough on the dance floor, so we've been practicing just a bit, but I don't want to scare him, so I pretend he'll simply sail on his feet.

"Eddie is a good dancer."

Well, your father will be glad to have his dance with his daughter, and hand you off to Eddie! How lucky both of us are that we have such wonderful daughters. It's no surprise that they've found wonderful men. Did I tell you that Clare Luce sent me a note, and she's planning a wonderful surprise for you.

"She told you what it is? What is it?"

It's something you might have a suspicion about, but I won't say more. Let's just say that it wouldn't require a whole shopping cart to bring it into the White House. Let me ask you, darling: don't you think long sleeves are best for my dress? I think they're always better, and with the dress length, I think long sleeves will be appropriate. New white gloves. I'll wear pearls. Have you decided on jewelry? Your sapphire and diamond engagement ring really is a dream come true. I guess it also takes care of that "something blue." I do agree with you that your hair pulled back will be elegant, and Priscilla can offer such good advice about a veil. I like things to be clear, including your sweet face on your wedding day.

"Julie and I wore white gloves to the Inaugural Ball, remember, Mommy?"

Oh, that picture where Julie is yawning? She would be the one yawning, being the youngest! I wore a sleeveless dress that night that I still have, but for a wedding, even a June wedding, I do think long sleeves will be best.

Your father is worried the roses won't be blooming in profusion, so he's spoken to one of the gardeners about bringing in extra rosebushes, if necessary! If I told him there was a magic dance he could do to ward off rain, *that* would be a way to get him to practice dancing! Shall we tell him that, just to have a bit of fun? Yes, let's pretend there's a special dance the President is supposed to do to ensure blue skies.

Mrs. Nixon Does Not Bend to Pressure

Two hundred thousand demonstrators are in Washington, May 3, 1971—I will never forget this day. They think they've thought things through, but they haven't. They don't understand the threat of Communism, and they don't understand that some of the finest minds in our country have thought things through and arrived at a very different conclusion than theirs. I know this much: Jerry Wilson is a patriot, and he's going to clear the streets and deal with these demonstrators who might find strength in numbers, though they'll never prevail because, individually, they are cowards. I'm going to do my part, too. I'm going to stay inside—not because I'm a coward, but because life goes on. Today the wives of the Ninety-second Congress will be having lunch here, and the noise of the buses might have to be drowned out by Beethoven. I only wish Dick could take time out of his busy schedule to be the person sitting at the piano.

Mrs. Nixon Hears a Name She Doesn't Care For

W ell, I've taken some flak for what I did, but no matter what I do, I'm the President of the United States, so I'm going to catch it every time. I started thinking about it and I thought, Why not give the Secret Service a runaround and call on Manolo—he's on my side, I know that—and the two of us could set off for one of the historic sites. Daytime, nighttime, it's a moving experience to visit the great monuments of Washington, D.C.

Manolo drove—I let him do that part—and when we got to the Lincoln Memorial, I felt the power of it all over again, and there were kids—sure there were; they were getting in some sightseeing before their big day of protesting—there were some kids on the steps, and one of 'em called out, "Hey! It's the President!" Well, how likely was that? But it wasn't so dark that they didn't stop what they were doing and see that it was the President, all right, but they still musta been surprised when I had a few things to say to them, because how often do you have an informal chat with the President? I'd told Haldeman to bring some of 'em to the White House, but then I thought, Why not go out there and show them I'm not afraid? Why not talk to 'em, show 'em that the President cares? I want this war over more than anybody, you can be sure of that.

Well, we did pretty well. I tried to tell them that it was a big world, and that travel was important. I tried to stop them from being so scared because, you understand, they weren't prepared to meet the President.

Manolo was very moved. He stood there staring up at Lincoln. I said to them that, sure, I could have avoided them, I could have been a coward, but I'm not a coward. How could they think I was, when I stood right there on the steps of the Lincoln Memorial? What they had to understand, though, was that I was making an effort, it wasn't something I had to do, it was never something I had to get into. The problem was bigger than the war, I told 'em. I said the blacks and the whites were separated, and it was a shame. That there had to be a way to communicate. And the Indians— what did they think about our treatment of them, or did they think about nothing but the Vietnamese people? Our treatment of the Indians was very shabby. Some of the Chicanos are worse off than the blacks, too, by the way.

It was dark, but I gestured. I told them, there are problems that need to be fixed, and some of the problems have to do with having messed up the planet we're living on. You know, it's my intention to clean things up. And I let 'em know it was my intention to end the war, too, bring the boys home, the boys and the girls. They were pretty impressed, you can be sure of that. They feel their oats when they're with their friends, but you get 'em alone, talk to them one-on-one, they understand that you care. That the President does. You know, that was a good idea I got from Nancy Dickerson to talk to the young people. Now, Pat, what's that look for? You can't be jealous of Nancy Dickerson! Anyway, if it makes you feel any better, I spoke to Helen Thomas, too, she knew I was heading off for the memorial, even if it was you-know-who who'd told me that I should go to them, I shouldn't just have Bob bring 'em to me. They were good kids. Kids that might grow up to be good Americans, once they've been set straight. Their president tried the other night. He got out there and talked to them. I told them, Go to Siberia, see what the folks were like there, see what they thought of living someplace like that. None of 'em probably has a dime to travel, but one day they might. We talked about a lot of things, and some of what I tried to say didn't go over, I know that, but still, it was good advice: go to them, don't have them come to you.

The President, Co-owner, with Mrs. Nixon, of Irish Setter King Timahoe, Called "King," Meets Elvis Presley, Known as "The King" but Called "Mr. Presley" by the President

King Timahoe, the Nixons' Irish setter, could be quite a pest. "King" disliked leashes, was disobedient, maniacally energetic, and spoiled. (Just ask Alexander Butterfield.) King wouldn't have tolerated being dressed up by the Lyndon Johnsons. (Though it is possible LBJ would have been amused if the staff person assigned to costume King Timahoe had been bitten. Johnson would have told this story happily at, say, Senate lunches.)

King Timahoe would have had a great time if anyone had let him into the room when Elvis visited. King always had a great time. Undisciplined. Fast. A dog who pretty much got his way. A spaceship could have flown in the window, and that would have added to the already bizarre fun. King could have barked at the spacemen. Peed on Elvis.

A little background information, since we all know Elvis met Nixon. (The photograph continues to astonish and is still often requested.) Elvis, in the doghouse (pun intended) with his wife and father for buying too many expensive guns and cars, ran away from Graceland. He flew around the country in a pretty manic state, breaking out in hives—from chocolate, his doctor maintained—or, more likely, in a rash that was a drug reaction.

Elvis had met Paul Frees, who was famous for doing voice-overs. Frees was the voice of the Pillsbury Doughboy. Americans heard Frees, though they never saw him. In any case, Frees—every bit as far-out as Elvis, but with less money—showed Elvis his credentials from the Bureau of Narcotics and Dangerous Drugs, and explained that cops let him go along with them on drug raids in Marin and even transport suspects to the police department in his Rolls-Royce. Frees was an "agent at large." Presley biographer Albert Goldman writes: "[Elvis] could go after the magic emblem of a federal narc! Gazing raptly at the document, as if he were beholding the Holy Grail or the Shroud of Turin, Elvis murmured: 'There isn't much that I've got that I wouldn't give to have one of those!'"

Thus began Elvis's journey toward President Nixon. On the plane to D.C., he met Republican Senator George Murphy (who was riding in coach; the stewardesses thought they might like to meet), and he asked if Murphy could help him with what he wanted to accomplish. It seems the senator could. In Washington, Elvis first called on the FBI, but J. Edgar Hoover was not available, and the person who did meet him turned him down. Elvis, however, had earlier left a note for President Nixon (6:30 A.M. A penny for the thoughts of the man in the guard's station who was approached by Elvis, already in full regalia). The note was relayed to the President's office, and, much to everyone's surprise, the President agreed to meet with him. At this time, President Nixon was just starting another bureau to deal with America's drug problem, so Elvis's arrival seemed fortuitous. Also, forty-one-year-old Egil

"Bud" Krogh had just started to work at the White House, and he thought the meeting would be a good idea.

Enter Elvis, clad in purple, with an enormous gold belt buckle he'd been given for drawing the biggest crowds ever to his shows in Las Vegas. With this he wore amber-tinted sunglasses and a cape. That's the picture everyone snickers over. Apparently reeling under the influence of drugs, Elvis asserted his patriotism (accurate, given how he construed patriotism), then began badmouthing the Beatles, who, he said, sang about drugs, were disheveled (no capes or purple outfits), and made money in America only to return to England, leaving behind corrupted youth, but not their money. Jane Fonda was also on Elvis's shit list. The Smothers Brothers. Elvis asked outright to be deputized; the President—who often said he had very little authority—floated the question to Bud Krogh, who wasn't experienced enough to know whether the President was hoping to hear him reply in the negative or in the affirmative. Soon, the only person who appears not to have been functioning at lunatic level, the Assistant Director of the FBI, who initially said no to Elvis (Elvis had suggested giving the FBI a "donation" of five thousand dollars), arrived at the White House with the documentation. Fast-forward to the future: hippies snorting, throwing darts into the official photo of Elvis and President Nixon.

That day, Elvis also gave a photograph of himself and his wife, Priscilla, to Nixon, as well as a photograph of his daughter in a baby bonnet. He held these things in one hand, while using the other to shake hands. Elvis also bestowed upon Nixon a Colt .45, which he'd earlier had to leave for safekeeping with the Secret Service. Nevertheless, President Nixon thanked him for this kindness. For his part, Nixon gave Elvis's two friends and bodyguards souvenir cuff links and a pin for each of their wives. RN said of the men: "Boy, you've got a couple of big ones here! I'll bet they take good care of you." No one in the Secret Service looked anything like Elvis's friends/bodyguards. Elvis replied in the affirmative. A photograph of the foursome was taken. For no reason I can understand, King Timahoe was not let into the Oval Office. During this time, it's likely King's thoughts were of catching a crow on the White House lawn, running away from valet Manolo Sanchez, or sleeping on expensive upholstery. What might have been the thoughts of Ollie Atkins, White House photographer? Or Egil "Bud" Krogh? And the thoughts of John Finlator of the FBI, the person who met Elvis and turned him down, only to be forced to show up later with exactly what the King wanted?

The fiction writer would of course be very interested in presenting everything from the POV of Mr. Finlator, token Sane Person. King the dog is just too easy; every day is pretty much the same for a high-strung dog who knows it will be indulged. My personal interest (of course) is in imagining what Mr. Nixon said to Mrs. Nixon that evening as they had dinner. It was December 21. Her mind would probably have been on Christmas. Any problems with groups scheduled to see the White House Christmas tree? Presents all ready for Dick and the girls? He might still have been thinking about the encounter with Elvis. He had said to Elvis: "You dress pretty wild, don't you?" Had the President ever heard Elvis's rendition of "Blue Christmas"? Whether he had or, more likely, hadn't, he had still let *Elvis* know that *he* knew things were a bit amiss, and he'd given him good advice, as well; he had assimilated this good advice and wanted to pass on his wisdom. He'd said to Elvis: "Never lose your credibility." That was the thing: you couldn't lose your credibility, or what would you have? Well, of course then you didn't have credibility, but how were you going to get it back, if you'd lost it? There was nobody coming behind you with a cart to pick up the credibility and put it in and deliver it back to your door, that was for sure. Mrs. Nixon would agree. She'd worked hard all her life, and she had credibility as a mother, and as a secretary, and as a teacher, and as the wife of Richard Nixon. Maybe it wasn't the thing to do, to have Haldeman sign off on Elvis's visit with a scrawled "You've got to be kidding" and Krogh . . . well, he was a youngster, and a bit inexperienced. Elvis was a man who went from rags to riches, just the way the song said, but who also went into the Army and served his country. He did do that, and it didn't do his career one bit of good, even if he did meet a teenager in Germany and wait for her to grow up; then, when it was a little more suitable, he married her. Anyway, better to have those people, patriots, dress up—better that real performers and patriots put on costumes than the hippies, who only wanted to cause everything to come crashing down so they could dance in the rubble in their feathers and their yak-fur vests.

"Dick! I was on the phone with Dolly. She's going to call you later."

"Everyone in the Christmas spirit? That's good. Hang up your stocking and the President will fill it if Santa doesn't. All of you hang them up. We want to see Fina's and Manolo's stockings hung. Has somebody arranged for Fina and Manolo to have their own stockings? Pat, I've got quite the story to tell you."

"What is it?"

"Well, you know, there was a note or something delivered to the White House today by Elvis Presley. I didn't see it. And that reminds me: he said he'd brought me a . . . well, another present I haven't looked into, either. Nice of him. Brought pictures of his wife—that teenager I read about in *Life*—*Life* or someplace like that. He came in to see me, quite colorful, I guess you could say, wearing a cape, all dressed up in purple velvet. Tall man. The thought was, it would be appropriate for the President to meet with him because I've told you about the Drug Enforcement Administration we're starting, putting a lot of money into that one. Well, here comes Elvis, and it must have made him pretty happy that I'd meet with him and have a picture taken. Ollie got that down. There I was with Elvis Presley, who said he'd come wanting to help us fight drugs, and so forth. Not a bad idea, someone the youngsters know."

"Elvis was here and I didn't know about it?"

"Oh, I guess I should have tried to call, should have thought of that, but you can't think about everything. Well, he was nice enough. Got a grudge against the Beatles. Make more money than he does, that sort of thing. Cuts into his sales, naturally. Not even from our country, they come here and throw their hair around like he swivels his hips, and all that. It might all be different now, I don't know. Our girls never cared about Elvis, and I'm just as glad we didn't have to have him sing at Julie's wedding. Probably we'd have had to get all new clothes for him, as well as the bride. Can't imagine Tricia would ever see anything in Elvis. Did Julie listen to his music? 'Heartbreak Hotel,' isn't that right? I remember a few things people might think I never noticed. The President is always watching. That's what they've got to believe. I guess we should have gotten him to sing that 'Heartbreak' song. Lighten up things a bit in the Oval Office. Some group of Korean kids coming through tomorrow, one of them with some problem or whatever. Haldeman's got it under control. I'll see them in the corridor and act surprised, rushing off somewhere. President's had an emergency. They'll get their picture with their teacher in the Oval Office. Unless, come to think of it, that was today, and it never happened. If it's tomorrow, maybe you could come for five minutes, give them a thrill, meeting Mrs. Nixon. You look pretty in any picture, too."

"What did you and Elvis talk about, Dick?"

"Oh, not so much. He seemed to think he could stop a concert and talk about how bad drugs were, things like that. I don't know if that would have worked. He did say something about how I was doing my job, he was doing his. Something that didn't really need saying, at least from my perspective. Gave me a picture of himself with his wife. She's pretty, but her hair was as high as her face. I guess if your hair stuck up that way, I'd know you'd seen a ghost. Mr. Lincoln walking around in the Lincoln Bedroom, instead of Mamie."

"Julie and Dolly might like a photograph of you with Elvis, Dick. Did Ollie think he got a good picture?"

"Well, he's sure to, because he's the White House photographer. Not an easy job, because you can't just order people around. They're nervous, being in the Oval Office. Don't want to be told 'Take a step to the left.'"

"I really like Ollie."

"Oh, I *know* you do."

"What do you mean?"

"I'm just kidding. I courted you, and I won you fair and square, didn't I? Well, everything like that is always *fair*, in love and war, as they say."

"I think they're waiting for us to stop talking so they can serve dinner, Dick."

"What if it was fillet of Ollie Atkins? That'd surprise you, I bet."
!!!!!!!!!!!

"Okay, well, maybe I am a little jealous, but you know me too well to worry. Or maybe I should say I know you too well to worry."

"Dick, can we go back to my idea about photographs for Christmas presents? You know, photographs are considered art now."

"Quicker than a portrait, that I can say. You look up and down the corridor, and you think of all of them—all important men, sitting one day and sitting the next for their portraits, and what do they have, in the end? A framed picture of themselves that might be good and might not be any good at all. Either way, who's really going to look at it? Though it is hung in the White House, I suppose."

"Have you ever seen photographs by Ansel Adams? He photographs very beautiful scenes. And Margaret Bourke-White? A woman did the first cover of *Life,* you know. They say she's fearless, she'll do anything to get the picture."

"Let's bring her into the White House and let her practice her art, then maybe we won't have to sit for our official portraits. It's sure to take plenty of time I don't have."

"I have a book I can put by your bed of Ansel Adams's photographs. One is of the moon rising over the mountains out in New Mexico, and it makes me want to go there tomorrow, it's so lovely."

"No time. I have to read a report Henry sent over."

"I'll speak to Ollie about making copies of you and Elvis for Julie and Dolly for Christmas."

"Well, maybe you can bring it up when you have your picture taken with the whatever they are, the Koreans. I'll have Haldeman call your office and tell you what the problem is there. Some kid with a problem—I can't remember."

"Maybe Elvis would like a picture for his daughter, Dick, don't you think?"

"She's a baby. Looks like she'd teethe on anything you handed her. Maybe she could come on over here and I could let her chew on Henry's latest report instead of me. Give her a special document saying she's First Baby."

"You know, Dick, today is the anniversary of F. Scott Fitzgerald's death."

"Is that right? What did he die of?"

"I think he had a heart attack."

"That wife was a lot of trouble, wasn't she? What are we having for dinner? Leftovers? Well, they wouldn't serve the President that. What wine are we drinking?"

"I was thinking about *The Great Gatsby,* and then someone on the radio mentioned that today was the day Fitzgerald had died in California, in 1940. I don't care for any wine. I wonder whether we shouldn't do something to honor his memory, once Christmas is over—I think there was a play based on his novel. We could have it performed at the White House."

"I don't know. Wasn't he spending all his time thinking about rich people? Not the kind of thing to celebrate here, if you know what I mean. We already receive too much criticism for not doing enough for the common man, or whatever it is our enemies think we should be doing, bowing down and scraping the ground for whatever we find down there, I suppose. Eating ants, if need be. Now, Elvis isn't a poor man, you can be sure of that. Maybe we should ask him to contribute to the campaign. Let me talk to Bebe about that. He'll know what's right."

Mrs. Nixon Reads The Glass Menagerie

The four characters of Tennessee Williams's *The Glass Menagerie* are a mother, her daughter, her son, and a "gentleman caller." In his notes describing them, Williams puts forth some of their inherent contradictions. Amanda, the mother, has "endurance and a kind of heroism, and though her foolishness makes her unwittingly cruel at times, there is tenderness in her slight person." Her daughter, afflicted with a bad leg, "is like a piece of her own glass collection, too exquisitely fragile to move from the shelf." Both female characters, damaged, live in their own realities. Tom, Amanda's son, who narrates, also embodies contradictions: he is a poet who works in a warehouse. Imagine being Jim O'Connor, invited to dinner: the daughter went to high school with Jim and has always secretly loved him; the mother, pining for the past and eager for any suitor; Tom, who yearns for independence, escapes these loonies any time he can and goes to "the movies."

Mrs. Nixon read this play to Julie, who was in high school, in 1965, though it was first performed twelve years earlier, so she might have already been familiar with it. Plays that dwelled on people's psychological aberrations were not usual then; selecting characters who had—as we would say now—arrested development were not usual, either. The palpable subtext of sexuality was pure Tennessee Williams: it could be read as a play that symbolically suggests incest. Tom, carelessly throwing his coat, breaks his sister's precious glass animals (hymen?), while Mom is muddled enough in her thinking to suspect that every man is her no-good, absent, drunken husband. She loves men, yet fears them. It's a Women versus Men play, with men representing wildness but the main female character wilder in her imaginings than any drunken lout.

Such extremes! Mrs. Nixon's own conflicts were her internal debate about what price she might be willing to pay in order to have freedom. She turned down a doctor's proposal of marriage. She left Whittier (and Mr. Nixon) in 1938, and when she returned, she did not call him. Yet once she decided on domestic life, she was by all accounts fiercely devoted to her family. Her daughters married young—though she could not have seen the future the night she sat reading to Julie. Gentlemen callers—one wants them, yet when they come to call, they bring with them their maleness. RN, though he played football, also played violin. Though he courted her with eloquently worded letters and what he thought of as unique gifts, he is remembered, along with LBJ, as among the most profane of our presidents. Though he wished freedom for her and for her to indulge her wanderlust, he repeatedly ran for public office against her wishes, and her travels took her to whatever event was listed in her daily schedule.

At the time she read to her daughter in 1965, it looked as if RN might have given up on politics. Defeated for governor of California, he went to New York to work in a law firm. Unlike Amanda Wingfield's husband in Williams's play, he never ran away from his family but rather put his own desires first, which interfered with their ability to function autonomously, unobserved by the press and the public.

What might Mrs. Nixon's reaction have been to *The Glass Menagerie*? She is quoted as saying, "I don't daydream, and I don't look back. I think what is to be will be, and I take each day as it comes."That's a big *it*—much determined by her husband's choices, which, like so many women of that era, she went along with. In the play, which the playwright conceived of as happening in memory, he used the device of words projected onto a screen that commented on the action by echoing or augmenting it: "Ha!"; "The crust of humility"; "Terror!" Mrs. Nixon needed no projected observations; the day's news about her husband often gave her that. No "Take that!" appeared over the helicopter that took them from the White House after his resignation, but she didn't know that was in her future. She had decided in her youth that she would not view her world as what might have been, but as holding great potential: she would accomplish her goal to finish college; she might be an actress; she would be a teacher; she decided to become a wife and mother. She had obvious intellect, skills, and talent, and nothing in Williams's play suggests Amanda Wingfield had those attributes. Amanda is passive, and believes in the fairy tale; Mrs. Nixon was active, and believed in working hard to create her own scenario. Both had an impenetrability, though. Both retained information that conflicted with their ideals. Amanda projects herself onto her daughter, while her daughter is a realist who sees what she is up against a bit cryptically, but pretty clearly. The Nixon daughters' identities so absorbed their father's determination that Tricia once wrote a note to her father urging him to go ahead and run again for public office because "if you don't run, Daddy, you really have nothing to live for." (The canary urged a return to the mine, because the person carrying the cage really wanted to reexplore it.)

Did Mrs. Nixon identify with a Southern belle dreamer? No. Did she sympathize with a mother doing everything possible to marry off her daughter? She, herself, would probably have done no such thing; also, she would have counted her blessings that her daughters, one brunette, one blond, both petite and feminine, had no reason not to be viable future wives. What did she think of the undercurrent of frustrated sexuality? Maybe best just to accept that someone was at "the movies" if that is what you are told. And the symbolism of Laura's glass animals—the unicorn being a particular favorite? Mrs. Nixon graduated cum laude; therefore, it seems likely that she would have understood the symbolism, perhaps known the legend of the unicorn, at least have realized that the unicorn was a fantasy that embodied things we needed to project onto it. Living in a fantasy, though? Not acceptable. The gentleman caller? She must have looked at him with some suspicion—not because he was calculating, because he is not, in the play. A bit naïve, but that's sometimes expected of men. Jim is already "taken," it turns out—he has a steady girlfriend. He kisses Laura, so might that be some beginning—a way for her to have better self-esteem? (He says he wishes this for her.) Or is he more drawn to her than he knows? Yes, there's the suggestion of that. Does he, perhaps, simply pity her? No, it seems more a question of unacknowledged attraction, or the fact that so many men do get away with misbehavior. Did the playwright's homosexuality figure in the play? (Both Williams and his sexually frustrated narrator are named Tom.)

Such a sad play, really: everyone caught by a lack of resources, whether they be financial or self-delusion as self-protection. Someone wanting to escape his constraints was limited by society's belief, along with his mother's, that, being a man, he would have to take care of his sister and also, by implication, of the other female in the family. What did you do, in those days, if you worked a pointless job—a man's job—but were nicknamed Shakespeare because you also loved poetry? He's complex, but he gets the fewest lines. But wait: he has his own power because he gets to narrate. Yet that's another self—a responsible self who has to tell the story, because the women could not; the narration also has to consider social constraints, as did the playwright. And no one ever answers him. In a variation of the device John Dos Passos used in *The 42nd Parallel* (1930), Williams adds to the play "real" information, in the form of real *Chicago Tribune* headlines—either stating the emotion in the scene (*"Où sont les neiges d'antan?"*), or giving us an image to correspond with a character's internal state, or to interject irony ("Screen image: The cover of a glamour magazine") that makes us contextualize what is happening differently. In *The Glass Menagerie,* memory is lit up onstage; it's as if we move forward in the present, while the past and the future light up the insides of our heads with their own commentary. Though artificial, the screen images are meant to approximate some physical state; like Freud—just starting to be popular—Williams wanted to deal with unstated inner conflicts.

The play is unsettling and was likely to have upset Mrs. Nixon in some ways. Did she read well, as the actress she had formerly been, or a bit haltingly, as a mother reading a curious text to a teenage daughter? Also, did she pause, slowed by her own awareness as a person familiar with inner conflict?

Amanda: "You modern young people are much more serious-minded than my generation. I was so gay as a girl!"

Mrs. Nixon (shrugging to avoid the implications of so many questions): "I guess I'm vindicated for going to the school of hard knocks."

At this point—her husband having been defeated for the presidency by John F. Kennedy—how much of her own life might Mrs. Nixon have seen in this claustrophobic play about Amanda and her

daughter, Laura? Mrs. Nixon, who prided herself on being prag-
matic, would not have easily identified with a dreamer. Amanda is
not the sort of character who'd pull herself up by her bootstraps,
or even wear anything as mundane as boots. I imagine the character in ballet flats: a slipper of shoe, worn for comfort by non-
ballerinas, the laces existing in romantic recall, even when the shoe
is abbreviated.

But what woman would not see something of herself in this
character, even if she was more functional? Less harmful. She is
a repository of some of society's expectations, almost a cauldron
of those things brought to boiling point, though we are certainly
meant to see her more as an exaggeration than as representative of
a type: a particularly misled, possibly somewhat piteous individual,
whose self-involvement ultimately punishes everyone in her orbit.

To try to answer my own question, I pose another: How often
do we judge characters, rather than understanding them? *Madame
Bovary* is much read, much taught, not because we approve of
adulterers (though we often do), but because this book is about an
individual whose surprisingly usual desires we might understand:
a person caught as much by her own temperament as by society's
rules. Who can read the sentence without feeling herself or himself
shiver, when her lover's coach lights the darkness, streaking away
from her as she stands in a room with her husband, the image
indelibly etching her lover's betrayal? There is no fainting in *The
Glass Menagerie,* but many of Laura's beloved glass animals end up
broken nonetheless—ruined hopes, but also perhaps punishment
of her mother by proxy?

Photo Gallery

1. Mrs. Nixon throwing horseshoes in the Rose Garden. An insomniac, Mrs. Nixon sometimes played a late-night game of horseshoes with the Secret Service agent assigned to her (L). Partially visible, with "Brontosaurus bone," King Timahoe (R).

2. An avid reader, Mrs. Nixon peruses a book by Norman Mailer.

3. Mrs. Nixon (L) greets schoolchildren touring the White House. David Eisenhower (R) adjusts his tie, to the amazement of this first grader.

4. Mrs. Nixon (L) and Rose Mary Woods (center) play Monopoly on a folding table in Mrs. Nixon's study. H. R. Haldeman (R) carries a Webster's dictionary from Mrs. Nixon's quarters.

5. The Nixons on Valentine's Day, holding a five-foot-high cardboard heart made by children at Dana-Farber Cancer Institute.

6. Entertaining Mrs. Khrushchev, Rose Garden, 1959. The two women grew close.

7. Sister Mary Alphonse Cochilla (L), Mrs. Nixon (center), and Julie Nixon Eisenhower (R). Rear: Alexander Butterfield (L), leaning toward Henry Kissinger (R).

8. A walk near the Jefferson Basin to view cherry blossoms with old friend Helene Drown (L), Tricia Nixon (R), and Reverend Billy Graham, partially visible, holding leash of King Timahoe.

9. New York City, Lord & Taylor, 1980.

10. First-grade honor student Jane Hill (L) joins Mrs. Nixon for "tea," served by White House pastry chef, Heinz Bender (R).

11. President Nixon (L) stands to applaud at Kennedy Center. Mrs. Nixon (R), rising.

Mrs. Nixon Thinks of Others

Romance is a funny thing to try to figure out, though it's probably easier when it's someone else's romance. It's hard to understand sometimes why you *are* drawn to someone. Your father thinks our marriage was meant to be. Impulsive of him, saying he'd marry me the first time we met! But at least there weren't two people being impulsive, because I needed a bit more time. I didn't want to give up my freedom. I've heard that one of those movie actresses gets a big department store in Los Angeles to open up late at night so she can shop. They do it, because when someone famous likes your store, chances are more and more people are going to show up. Do you think we should ask the Secret Service to rouse the sales staff at Woodies and turn on the lights for you and me, and we could try out some of the new fall styles and give your father a big surprise with the news we'd been midnight shopping?

We should have some handouts for our special tour. Some inspirational thoughts from the Founding Fathers, mimeographed? Maybe an inspirational saying from Jefferson or Washington? Some people get cuff links or other things from your father's desk drawer, but this group won't be going in, so maybe we should have a nice little memento for them. Maybe a letter opener with the presidential seal and inside the envelope a few smart things said by Lincoln, or General Eisenhower. Maybe it would be good to remind them of a few things men of distinction thought to say, rather than their spending their time listening to Bob Dylan.

They say he took his name from the poet. Well, I ditched Thelma. When you think about it, so many people changed their names as a prelude to living their lives another way.

In what book? That's interesting, I didn't realize the Great Gatsby made up his last name. Well, there you go. Might have been a little immodest if he came up with "Great," though. Oh, I'm being silly, I know. I'm just so happy to have my daughters curled up with me here, and not to be on an airplane. It makes me very proud to know you'll be conducting tours of the White House tomorrow. You be sure to let your father know how things go, but don't tell him anything that's troublesome, because he needs a bit of cheering up. Not that we've ever told him every little thing that's gone wrong. It's life, so things go wrong!

Well, for one thing, that book I read to you when you were little. *A Child's Christmas in Wales.* You loved it. Maybe not more than *The Night Before Christmas,* but your eyes got big as saucers and you just loved that book.

I'm keeping you up. They'll have finished vacuuming by now, my loves, and you should get some sleep. We have more noise and interruptions to put up with than people could imagine, don't we? Wouldn't it be grand to open the windows and hear the ocean or to hear the birds singing in the trees? I saw the biggest crow on the lawn the other day. Just one, all alone. I watched for a while, expecting a whole bunch of them to land, but the crow just went pecking along all by itself, and then I had to go to a meeting.

That color is beautiful on you, Dolly. You should wear it more often. I don't think it *is* a strange color, though the pastel nightgown has an even softer hue, doesn't it? It's beautiful, and so are you. Good night, Dolly.

A Home Movie Is Made About
Mrs. Nixon in China

"Well, all right, I'll try. One of those guys from NBC with a long name I can't remember . . ."

"Fred Flamenhaft."

"That's it. Well, Fred came along to the dinner at the Peking Roast Duck Restaurant, and after the dinner there were quite a few toasts."

"Mao-tai brandy."

"That's right. You certainly read the information I gave you carefully, Julie. I just held the drink to my lips. I didn't want to give the appearance of not toasting."

"You'd never do that."

"Of course I wouldn't. Well, Fred wasn't the first to give a toast, he was pretty much the last, and when his turn came, you know what he did? He toasted the duck! He said, 'I don't give a damn what you all said, I've just had the best meal of my life, and I toast the duck!' It gave us a good laugh."

"You don't think President Nixon might have spoken to him later about cursing?"

"Oh, Dick has a fine sense of humor. He knew it was all good fun."

"Flamenhaft is a funny name, isn't it?"

"People can't help the names they're born with. If he'd decided to call himself that, that would be another matter. Are we about done?"

"I'd like to ask just one or two more questions. As I mentioned, this will be edited, and it will have your approval."

"All right. What else?"

"What you should do when you're traveling and you're in another country and you're served something you can't eat. Like something slimy."

"I grew up on a farm, remember. I'm not a vegetarian or someone who won't try most things once."

"What if it was really repulsive, like some gray, mushy fish?"

"Julie, as I've taught you girls, you delicately push it a bit to the side and eat the other things."

"Watching the acupuncture made you squeamish, didn't it?"

"Yes, it did. But the needles didn't leave any scars, I noticed. And that is their way. They've done this for centuries. I think we've talked enough now."

"This is going to be the most impressive home movie project ever: interviews with all the important people who went with Daddy to China."

"I'm not going to approve some of these questions and answers, you know. Now I would appreciate it if you could get that camera out of my face."

Mrs. Nixon Gets the Giggles

I thought Lady Bird would be the one to cut up, but that young man was so proper, I just couldn't help myself. "We'd like to have tea with the Queen," I said, and of course he couldn't comply. There was no way he could. He just didn't know what to do. What if the Queen had been there, and she'd said, "Yes, of course, one does so wish to see Pat and Lady Bird." I don't suppose she would have said it that way, she'd say "Mrs. Nixon" and "Mrs. Johnson," and her butler would have said, "Yes, mum, most certainly, mum." Or is "mum" just the Queen Mother? I need a briefing about the English royal family. We could call Henry in. *Henry* is a man who dearly loves an important late-night briefing. Ha ha ha ha ha ha ha ha ha ha ha ha ha ha ha.

Cathedrals

"From the moment of taking office, when he promised, in his first Inaugural Address, to build 'a great cathedral of the spirit' and unify the nation, to the spring of 1973, when he had Senate Minority Leader Hugh Scott announce on his behalf, 'We have nothing to hide,' he filled the air with empty and intentionally misleading phrases—phrases that in both tone and content were without relation either to each other or to the actions of his Administration," writes Jonathan Schell, in *The Time of Illusion*.

Nixon did a lot of his own speech writing, but it's equally probable he was reading the words of a speechwriter when he made his metaphor about the "cathedral of the spirit." That doesn't sound much like RN to me. The idea of citizens being part of a group—even a group that met in church—would have set off his paranoia. Also, he didn't tend to think in terms of "the spirit." In any case, Schell jumps on him for this phrase.

Years later, Raymond Carver wrote one of his most famous stories, "Cathedral." It, too, is about a cathedral of the spirit, but Carver was one for understatement. The word *cathedral* signifies well enough. Say the word to a minister, and he or she would prob-ably conjure up the architectural building. Say it to the American public, and they would probably hear it as mere fancy rhetoric. Say it to a writer, and there's every chance they'd conjure up Carver's story.

The story concerns an unusual but plausible event: one evening, a woman whose friend is blind (absent for years, though she has kept in touch with him) finds out he is going to visit. She intro-duces him to her husband.

Carver depends on certain things. Among them: our own uneasiness upon meeting a blind man. He must also realize that by the time he writes "Cathedral," late in his career, his readers are educated to the way he inflects a story, and to the way subtext almost becomes text itself: characters speak to keep emotions at bay; subtext fights to rise to the surface and wreak havoc. Meta-phorically, there's often a wild animal in Carver, and the cage that contains it never seems very secure.

The wife turns on a recording sent from the blind man to her, but Carver sees to it that just when the man's words might reveal something important, his sentence does not conclude. Rather, they all stop listening. It's a cliff-hanger, and the readers are left at the edge. What kind of story has the wife previously told the blind man about her husband? We don't know, and if the husband has curiosity (rather than dread), he decides that not knowing is better than asking the question.

As the story progresses, people seem to relax—or, at least, have the opportunity to do that. The wife leaves the two men alone, and when she reenters the room, she promptly announces she's going to fall asleep, and does. When her robe falls in a way that reveals her body, the husband at first reaches out to close it, then, instead, flips it open. Carver allows the husband to literally finger text and subtext in this gesture. As time passes, the TV is turned on: "Something about the church and the Middle Ages . . . was on the TV. Not your run-of-the-mill TV fare. I wanted to watch something else. I turned to the other channels. But there was nothing on them, either. So I turned back to the first channel and apologized." The blind man says it's fine: "It won't hurt me to learn something tonight. I got ears," he says.

The blind man can't envision a cathedral. He knows about how they're built. He knows the factual things, but they don't excite his imagination. It is his idea, finally, that his host draw a cathedral on a piece of paper. The paper selected is utilitarian: large, because it's a grocery bag, but not exactly something to accommodate a work of art. This is the world of Raymond Carver, though, so no one is an *artist*. Neither is an artistic depiction necessary; what's necessary is that the two men bond as the husband attempts to draw, for the first time (his own house metamorphoses into a cathedral), and the blind man begins to learn something meaningful. The TV show continues.

"I said, 'They're statues carved to look like monsters. Now I guess they're in Italy. Yeah, they're in Italy. There's paintings on the walls of this one church.'"

"'Are those fresco paintings, bub?' he asked, and he sipped from his drink.

"I reached for my glass, but it was empty. I tried to remember what I could remember. 'You're asking me are those frescoes?' I said. 'That's a good question. I don't know.'"

The notion of "frescoes" *is* a good one. It tells the reader the blind man has a certain level of sophistication. Perhaps also that he's trying to get the upper hand with his guide. It introduces an important concept: frescoes are painted directly on a wall of wet plaster—quickly, with the artist having almost no ability to redo anything. The process is very tactile, it happens quickly, and the artwork has a freshness that painting done over a long period of time may lack. One subtext of this question (along with testing the husband's knowledge and sophistication) is: is the painting spontaneous? Because the husband and the blind man are two people who are clearly plodding along, dope smoking or not. They are both going through the motions. Arduously. On television (which only the husband can *see*), we realize that, unless the husband has been told (*his* sense of hearing matters here, too), he isn't able to say whether he's looking at frescoes or at oil paintings, a more drawn out medium. The question, though, and the issues it raises, hangs in the air. When the husband metamorphoses into an artist of sorts, he's speaking words about cathedrals, but he's also drawing—creating them. He finds his efforts inadequate: "I'm just no good at it." In part because he admits some vulnerability (lack of talent), but also because spontaneity is about to burst forth finally, the blind man asks a question: is his host "in any way religious"? The answer: "I guess I don't believe in it. In anything. Sometimes it's hard. You know what I'm saying?" Notice the echo of *it* ("I'm just no good at it" and "I guess I don't believe in it"). *It* means a lot—so much that the shorthand is deliberately used to gloss over the deep significance of an *it* that is so vast, it is impossible to define. Carver uses words judiciously. One could think that he had a small vocabulary—or that his characters do, and he's trying to represent them faithfully. The meaning of a word as vague and seemingly minor as *it* shifts in Carver. There's not much that doesn't shift like sand in a windstorm in a Carver story—or become a sinkhole.

There's a sense of exhilaration near the end of "Cathedral." The tables are turned, and the blind man, Robert, is instructing the husband—and also telling the husband to keep his eyes closed. His hands atop the husband's, they have been drawing their cathedral.

Significantly, the husband does not want to open his eyes to look at the finished drawing. The suggestion is that what is seen might be (must be?) either inadequate or, however complete, still lacking. Paradoxically, in putting himself in the blind man's position and keeping his eyes closed, the husband sees more and more inwardly, until—after this night of having created facades—he says: "But I didn't feel like I was inside anything." Earlier, of course, he's been in his routine. He's been inside his house, inside his life, watching TV. But through imagination, he's escaped. Talk hasn't done it. Neither has smoking pot. He concludes, in the last line of the story—which is quintessentially Carveresque in stating the inexpressible in a banal way, while making the reader infer the layers of underlying inexpressible complexities. The character says: "It's really something."

The story is also about creation—about fiction, about being an artist. It's easy to see the husband and the blind man as opposites, yet opposites that inform one another. The yearning is sexual, and it's also aesthetic, and it's also a moment escaped into, we don't know for how long. The story is a paradigm of the artistic process. Something greater than the will of the two men is taking its course (Beckett); something is happening, but (as Bob Dylan sings, sneeringly) "you don't know what it is, do you, Mr. Jones?" The story is full of religious undertones, as is much of Carver's writing. Art aspires to the sublime. In this case, as with Flannery O'Connor's Misfit, the most unlikely character is, ironically, the one who provokes the reader's deepest (most spiritual) belief.

Something of grandeur—something vast and noble and beautiful—is being invoked if we hear about a "cathedral of the spirit," as if the spirit can be touched and built upon, as if something new and important will exist, something we can point to, if only we will envision it, if only (like Peter Pan) we *believe*. Lyndon Johnson was a bit vague when he spoke emphatically of "a great society"—and anyway, he said we already had it: we just had to recognize it. Kennedy had Camelot, but that was in-house talk that was eventually heard by others, an inflated sense of personal nobility. Nixon and the cathedral of the spirit . . . it's doubtful it was something he truly believed. It just sounded good, and he was a man who liked formality and for things to be substantial—which was synonymous with impressive. He cared very much about how things *looked*.

Mrs. Nixon didn't think metaphorically. She did, however, think for herself—even if she thought well within cultural conditioning. Imagine that RN asked her to conjure up a "great cathedral of the spirit" that would unify a divided, chaotic America. To her, a "great cathedral of the spirit" would probably be quite abstract. She seemed to live in the here and now—or tried to. At least, she tried very hard not to live in the past. Imaginative speculation? Mrs. Nixon? There wouldn't have been much sense in asking her opinion on that.

Still, she was not without the ability to imagine. She accompanied RN on his trip to Russia, and RN himself wrote in his diary: "As we looked at the sea, there was a three-quarter moon. Pat said that since she was a very little girl, when she looked at the moon, she didn't see a man in the moon or an old lady in the moon—always the American flag. This, of course, was years before anybody ever thought of a man actually being on the moon or an American flag being there. She pointed it out to me and, sure enough, I could see an American flag in the moon. Of course, you can see in the moon whatever you want to see."

Together, the Nixons might have had a moment not unlike the one in the Carver story where the characters sense that something ineffable eludes them. RN seems unimpressed when he is invited to share his wife's version of what can be seen on the moon; he could have wondered at the fact that two Americans in Russia saw their flag plastered across the moon, or that neither of them was moved to see a man there, as others did. RN misses a chance to share some uncertainty or humility with his wife; they avoid the subtly life-changing intuition that Carver's two men share. Using a cliché to dismiss his wife's imagination, he reinforces his pride in his hardheaded common sense. We see RN bluntly cutting off a realization that "it's really something." (On seeing Hangchow, Nixon called on what might have been his highest praise, as close as he got to true wonder: "It looks like a postcard with those mountains in the background.")

What Did Mrs. Nixon Think of Mr. Nixon?

T hat's the question. She did not want a public life, so, beyond a certain point, she didn't want RN to be involved in politics at all. He reentered the race despite her desires. Consider this: She was an actress. I'm not suggesting that, because she appeared as Daphne Martin in the play *The Dark Tower*, her character described as "a tall, dark, sullen beauty of twenty," Mrs. Nixon glided onstage at the Republican National Convention with equal ease, being—as I would describe her—"a woman of average height, light-haired, attractive but no beauty, in her forties." But, because of training, she was accustomed to ignoring stage fright and simply proceeding. Also, the plays she had acted in or was aware of, such as *The Glass Menagerie*, had some things in common, and it seems reasonable to assume the play's ideas affected her, as well. Our literature defines us, and, in those days, I think plays were generally considered more important than they are now.

Mrs. Nixon also had a role in the movie version of *Becky Sharp* (though she was cut out of the final version). *Becky Sharp* was published with the subtitle "A Novel Without a Hero"—a common concept now, but less usual when Thackeray published his novel. Becky's rise in society has to do with climbing the social ladder, marrying well, traveling. She is primarily interested in being a well-off, notable person. (There is still some debate about whether Thackeray wanted to suggest she actually murdered another character: an illustration done by the author shows her behind a curtain with a vial of poison and uses the word "Clytemnestra," though this was later deleted.) Again: murder, or intimations of murder. A woman having to work within social constraints, but willing to do any number of things, go any number of places, to get ahead. *Becky Sharp* has entered the vocabulary to describe a particular kind of ambitious woman, the same way Kato Kaelin awakened people to the fact that there are people who are *not exactly* servants, who have vaguely defined roles in wealthy people's lives while sponging off them.

The Dark Tower is set in the France of the Sun King, and Act I requires two props of Richelieu: "Richelieu hat and gloves under glass dome" and "Picture—Richelieu—on stairs." World War II is the backdrop for *The Glass Menagerie*. All have in common families as the dominant social reality, subtexts of unhappiness or even despair, the theme of unrequited love (Dobbin, in Thackeray, is the most remembered character, after Becky herself), as well as the idea of the enterprising woman who takes charge of her own life— or its flip side: the woman or women (*The Glass Menagerie*) who literally or metaphorically collapse, done in by their frustration.

As people know, if their older relatives lived through the Depression, that generation learned to live frugally and never forgot doing without; therefore, they do not make long-distance phone calls (except sometimes to report a death) and have a very strange reaction when looking at restaurant menus. Thelma Ryan's family was poor. Her father died of tuberculosis contracted in the mines. They had barely enough of anything. There was, however, a piano that had come with the farm Mrs. Nixon's parents bought, and in mentioning her grandmother's piano playing, Julie Nixon Eisenhower remembers the following song: "The music she most often chose was the plaintive song of the Indian maid Red Wing, who '. . . loved a warrior bold, this shy little maid of old. But brave and gay, he rode one day to battle far away.'"

Lyrics like these get instilled in children's minds: the nobility involved, but also the sadness and inevitability of the beloved going off to war. Every girl must identify with Red Wing (unless she is the one doing the leaving—and those song lyrics don't leap to mind). Mrs. Nixon was left alone by people she loved (who left her by dying). Mr. Nixon left, too, enlisting in World War II and going to the South Pacific, as Red Wing's warrior departed long before. Our civilization carries countless variations on the theme: every woman was Penelope, every man Ulysses. Women were expected to be strong. Mrs. Nixon, like so many wives, wrote her husband daily and worked for the war effort. She was patriotic, recognizing our flag, rather than the man-in-the-moon face, in the moon, and she could not understand young people who didn't share her version of patriotism, who marched against the war in Vietnam, who waved signs at the White House urging an end to the war, who wore crazy-looking clothes not because they were poor but because they had enough money to cut holes in their jeans when they didn't have time to wear out the material, who had enough time to tie-dye T-shirts into smashed kaleidoscopes of color because they didn't have to do the weekly wash, and to take over universities in their copious spare time.

Youths' counterculture never made sense to a lot of people of Mrs. Nixon's generation. Perhaps if she had reflected on her reading of, and performance in, plays, such rebellious youths would have become more accessible. Becky Sharp fights her way out of society's expectations, and the women in *The Glass Menagerie* pay a terrible price for not questioning the prescribed roles of men and women. It might have helped Mrs. Nixon to see Mr. Nixon as a Williamsesque "gentleman caller"; not necessarily reliable, or who he claimed to be, and certainly not a knight in shining armor. When she resisted him initially, it was because she was interested in going against the script and making a life for herself: to act; to travel; to do whatever seemed compelling. Socially, things were beginning to open up a bit—especially because women were needed to go to work during the war—so there was a little less emphasis on marriage and motherhood. Though she had to work, she must still have thought that she had quite a bit of autonomy. Didn't Becky Sharp and the other women she knew from plays?

It was to her workplace that Mr. Nixon sent the engagement ring. Instead of her putting it on and dancing in circles, we have Julie Nixon Eisenhower's report of the gift's recipient: "For a few seconds, she stared at it blankly. All morning she had anticipated her future husband's arrival, the unveiling of the ring, the romantic moment when he would put it on her finger. And, now, here it was, in a May basket. Impulsively, she shoved the offering a few inches away from her." Another teacher is described as entering the classroom: "Look, you are going to put on that ring and right now." How much did Mrs. Nixon intuit about her future husband by the gesture he made? Did she want more romance (his presence), or merely a more conventional scenario (a personal presentation), or might she have wanted none of it and reacted spontaneously in a very significant way? This possibility is skipped over, as if anyone might have had such a reaction.

A writer would see such a response as a not-so-subtle gesture that expressed something important about the character. Depending on the story, her actions could be a moment's faltering, or fear mixed with happiness, or—more interesting—a gesture that is unexpected, even by the character.

Writers may give the impression that their characters are truly surprised by something, though quite often they're the ones who are startled into a new consciousness. Flannery O'Connor, whose essays contain some of the most sensible things ever written about writing, says it this way (she is commenting on her story "Good Country People," in which the character's wooden leg is stolen by a Bible salesman): "This is a story that produces a shock for the reader, and I think one reason for this is that it produced a shock for the writer." Subconsciously, things are working in the writer's mind as the writer acts as scribe, transcribing events. If something totally unexpected happens in real life, it can't be revised except in the story that is *told* about the occurrence. A storyteller can omit things, decide on a different starting point, play things for laughs, or emphasize certain elements of the story to elicit the desired effect. But mostly, since the fiction so many write is already at some distance from the actual, writers retain a superstitious respect for what was somehow told *to* them, rather than *by* them.

In telling Julie the story of receiving the ring, Mrs. Nixon is not writing fiction, exactly, but giving what she thinks of as an honest account of how something happened. She depends upon her daughter's not asking for clarification (Julie doesn't), trusting not that the action will speak for itself, but that it will *not* speak for itself. Leaving us with the words of someone essentially outside the situation is a clever way to deflect attention from the main event. History—time—already informs the person hearing the story: Mrs. Nixon did marry him, so the implication is that her friend gave good advice. But a fiction writer could not include the scene as recounted without realizing that the action of the story abruptly stopped.

The fiction writer could, quite possibly, think the character's response to receiving the ring was a much too obvious moment of real, unverbalized feeling asserting itself and try to rewrite the scene to be more subtle. I sometimes find myself in the position of emphasizing things not by raising the volume, but by muting the sound. This is where breaks in the text, such as white space, come in, where asterisks are as frightening as asteroids coming at Planet Earth, where little things retain their size, but gain great weight, in falling.

What happened in those moments between Mrs. Nixon's seeing the ring and the friend's walking into the classroom, seeing the basket, seeing the ring, and putting it on Mrs. Nixon's finger?

That's where we may have our answer, but no one's talking.

Questions

A friend, Radici restaurant, Portsmouth, N.H., June 2007: "Do you identify with Mrs. Nixon?"

My mother, in the nursing home, 2008: "Are you kidding?"

Salesclerk, Lyrical Ballad Bookstore, Saratoga Springs, N.Y., July 2007: "Some *Life* magazines, huh? Look at that [Tricia Nixon Cox, on the cover, in her bridal dress]! You know, I saw Mrs. Nixon once, in Washington. At the Kennedy Center. She was so thin. (Long pause.) It wasn't her fault."

The Nixons as Paper Dolls

Tom Tierney has done a number of books of paper dolls. He gives a brief biography of his subjects and draws figures to cut out ("Do not cut out white area between arm and body"). There is a diagram of how to make stands for them. It has fold lines and tabs and measurements. Its construction is something I could never accomplish, though my husband could make the stand while also drinking coffee, talking on the telephone, painting, and listening to music. Like many writers, I am preoccupied with the horizontal world—reading books—so paper dolls don't have to be upright for me to enjoy them. Neither do I think the book was really intended as an opportunity to cut out paper dolls. It's a riff on coloring books and cutouts, aimed at adults. The book is funny because it pretends to be something it isn't: fun for children. The humor is tongue-in-cheek; it's a diversion for the audience that involves real, historic figures, deflated and made laughable by their presentation as things a child would play with. It's the sort of thing Mr. Nixon always feared: being disparaged, somehow diminished, "dissed." There were plenty of rolled eyes and derogatory terms behind his back, though to his face he remained Mr. President.

A friend gave me the book of paper dolls long before I thought of writing about Mrs. Nixon. I laughed, flipped through, then put it away and forgot about it. When I was writing this book, I opened a file drawer and there it was, tossed in among the many uncategorizable items; it was probably a sign of mental health not to know how to file them. It has a plaintive quality. No embellishments, the figures as slender as they were in real life, with Mr. Nixon's slight shoulder slouch well drawn. In a way, we're always dressing up and dressing down political figures. The press takes note of anything out of the ordinary, whether it be a belt buckle or a slightly different haircut. As a public figure, Mrs. Nixon knew she was being scrutinized, and her response was to scale everything down to make sure her clothes were never worthy of comment: conservative; well pressed; well chosen. She hoped to hide behind her attire, to seem proper and invisible at the same time. This is how she proceeded generally as First Lady. She did things behind the scenes when possible. She did not search out the camera lens like Princess Di. She appeared proper—always proper. She let herself be defined by her acts, whether she was a representative of the United States or simply a housewife visiting schoolchildren. She wanted to be able to do what she did more or less unnoticed. Hillary Clinton, perhaps the most restyled First Hair ever, ultimately indicated insecurity, rather than perfectionism. When you really can't decide on a post-headband hairstyle, it becomes a problem. Mrs. Nixon wasn't that way. She opted for protective coloration. She was the generic president's wife, suited, modestly slipping into sensible shoes, conservatively coiffed. Yet her husband, when asked what he would like for his wife's birthday, responded: "A walk on the beach, with the breeze in her hair." He knew that she loved the breeze, representing freedom.

Since rediscovering my Nixon paper dolls, I've made a plan.

I imagine a centerpiece on my dining room table: some small vases of summer flowers and a few Nixons standing around: Dick in a "midnight blue" tuxedo; Pat in the blue, ankle-length outfit she wore in Liberia in 1972. The matching blue headdress swirls upward like one of those twirling candles that are thought to be an improvement on simple vertical candles. Flanking the demitasse cup filled with short-stemmed cosmos would be Julie, wearing a knee-length green and white dress with a sash at the waist (green) and edging at the hem (green), along with modest heels (green). This was the dress she wore for her last Christmas in the White House, and it is very neat and proper. Her husband, David, who had been called to duty, wore his naval uniform. He could be standing beside Julie with the saltshaker lined up beside him in a gesture toward military formation. Moving to the pepper grinder—rather formidable in case anyone started to list to starboard—we would see older daughter Tricia (very appropriate, in this context, as Dolly) and Edward Cox. Tricia, a bit in the background (she was reticent about public appearances), would be wearing a pink dress with matching headband and shoes, and her husband would have on the formal morning suit with striped pants that he wore to his wedding. There's no middle ground for Edward Cox: we get him either in his underpants or in his wedding suit. Alas, there are no paper-doll pets, so neither the poodle nor the Irish setter can be with them.

Even *more* amusing might be the depictions of them in their underwear. There are notes on the underwear, informing us that "the President and Mrs. Nixon are shown in underwear typical of the period." Mr. Tierney seems to have had a bit of editorial fun with the underwear of Edward Cox. He wears "a paisley-patterned knit A-shirt with matching knitted briefs, typical of the 'Peacock Revolution' of the sixties when bold patterns and vivid colors became fashionable for men's undergarments." A real peacock would blanch. The underwear, in shades of dark purple paisley, suggests fluorescent sperm swimming under a microscope, inside a lavender petri dish. He wears matching dark purple socks.

Laughing at the Nixons. Haven't we all done that? The little Nixons in all their sadly recognizable finery, standing around some tabletop, put there by someone who can't even get it together to buy apples and place them in a bowl for a centerpiece, but who has silver candelabra (inherited) and sterling silver salt dishes (inherited)—a writer who has taken the time to place cutouts of the Nixon family in their underwear amid summer flowers.

Writers like to do funny things decorating tabletops. You would not see such decorations in *Elle Decor*. What writer owns an obelisk? No writer I've met has any small topiary. They might have a DVD of *Edward Scissorhands*, but topiary has negative associations because it is so often plunked on tables so you can easily talk around the trunks during tedious fund-raisers. Florists go crazy when told to decorate tables at which writers will sit. It seems to bring out their most frighteningly whimsical thoughts, with icing that spells out the name of the author's book piped around containers that hold noise blowers, or disposable cameras placed on the tables so the authors can take candid photos as their fellow writers set to serious drinking (who wouldn't?). In their homes, some writers are rather discreet and have on the table one beautiful object, or candles. Some do have a vase of flowers. But you'll also find a collection of fifties clip-on earrings in a little Limoges dish, or a geode on a tiny stand, and of course unpaid bills. Poets have stones. Little plastic animals are common, pushed into position sniffing each other's backsides. Among writers, high seriousness does not preside at table. And as any hostess knows, putting out little things that can be fiddled with (plastic gorilla atop salt dish, elevated to confront miniature pewter water buffalo) makes people feel at ease and breaks the ice. Writers, generally, either are very good cooks or do not cook at all. Little place cards (swiped from Important Occasions: "Mr. DeLillo"; "Ms. Nesbit") can be oh so merry, though they do not mark the places of people attending.

The following is a list of other truths about writers, rarely discussed:

1. They take souvenirs of Important Evenings for their "mother." This is like taking leftovers home for the "dog." Of course, some mothers do get the souvenirs and some dogs do get the scraps. However, it is not likely.

2. If they find a copy of Richard Yates's *Eleven Kinds of Loneliness,* they buy it. It is as if they've found a baby on the front step. They peek inside, examine the dog-earing, the marginal scribbles. Or perhaps it's a clean copy, which carries its own kind of sadness. In either case, they embrace it, though they already have multiple copies. Those are irrelevant to the one they would be abandoning if they left the book behind. This is a hostess gift you can give any fiction writer, guaranteed to delight her even though she already has it. Regifting becomes an act of spreading civilization.

3. It makes the writer's day if he or she can include the opinions of a truly stupid character or text in the story, punctuating those announcements with exclamation points, which are the icing on the cake. This situation is to be found in novels, too, but novelists are less likely to be immensely flattered if you have noticed their needle in the haystack(!). For particularly adept and judicious uses of the exclamation point, see the works of Joy Williams and Deborah Eisenberg.

4. Without these things, many contemporary American short stories would grind to a halt: fluorescent lights; refrigerators; mantels. They are its gods, or false gods. In that it is difficult to know Him, these stand-ins are often misspelled.

5. Poets go to bed earliest, followed by short story writers, then novelists. The habits of playwrights are unknown.

6. Writers are very particular about their writing materials. Even if they work on a computer, they edit with a particular pen (in my case, a pen imprinted BOB ADELMAN); they have legal pads about which they are very particular—size, color—and other things on their desk that they almost never need: scissors; Scotch tape. Few cut up their manuscripts and crawl around the floor anymore, refitting the paragraphs or rearranging chapters, because they can "cut" and "paste" on the computer. As a rule, writers keep either a very clean desktop or a messy one. To some extent, this has to do with whether they're sentimental.

7. Writers wear atrocious clothes when writing. So terrible that I have been asked, by the UPS man, "Are you all right?" An example: stretched-out pajama bottoms imprinted with cowboys on bucking broncos, paired with my husband's red thermal undershirt (no guilt; he wouldn't even wear such a thing in Alaska) and a vest leaking tufts of down, with a broken zipper and a rhinestone pin in the shape of pouting lips. Furry socks with embossed Minnie Mouse faces (the eyes having deteriorated in the wash) that clash with all of the above.

If the Nixons came to my house in Maine, they would be overdressed. Thin people, they would be cold on the back porch and sweaters would have to be brought out, some quite ratty. Music they did not recognize would be playing on the boom box in the kitchen. (Music I do not recognize, either.) There would be a lot of food, but they wouldn't be able to figure out the majority of the ingredients. There would be mismatched plates, and wine would be served in the wrong glasses. The ice bucket would be holding a plant, rather than ice. The view would be of a lovely field that is zoned commercial, with only two restrictions on its use as a business: no head shops; no auto dump. (Recently, we were lucky enough to turn aside plans for a proposed twenty-four-hour lighted storage facility with razor wire, but only on a technicality: the turn onto our street is so dangerous, the sight lines so deficient, that such a business would pose a liability.) The Nixons could take off their shoes, as we do, and when it was time for dinner, they could sit at our square picnic table, with its so-bad-it's-hip sixties tablecloth (more sedate than Edward Cox's underwear, but still pretty deranged). I would of course know to pour superior French wine for Mr. Nixon, though the rest of us could drink plonk.

My mother used to rock me to sleep. One of the songs was about paper dolls: "I'm gonna buy a paper doll that I can call my own, a doll that other fellows cannot steal." She had quite a repertoire of old songs. A nice voice, too. Once, she got so enthusiastic we rocked over backward. That same rocker—the one she'd sat in while pregnant, the one she'd later rocked me in—is still rocking on my back porch, badly in need of repair.

That might be a conversation starter. At least, with Mrs. Nixon.

Mrs. Nixon Is Taken on a Drive, 1972

"A Howard Johnson's. We've eaten at Howard Johnson's. They have good ice cream. It reminds me how much I loved ice cream when I was a girl."

"In a cone?"

"Oh, yes. Strawberry."

"I liked ice cream sundaes when I was a kid, without whipped cream. I never developed a taste for that."

"And that's the building? All of that, over there?"

"Yes, ma'am."

"There were some Cubans, and some other people?"

"Uh-huh."

"It's quite large, isn't it?"

"Yes."

"The group of them got together and went there at night. And broke in."

"That's apparently what happened."

"That person cut in front of us without signaling."

"Passed on the right, too. That's against the law."

"I saw an accident on Constitution Avenue a few weeks ago. Someone hit another car from behind at a red light. I kept walking. I didn't think they'd need a witness because with that sort of accident it's obvious what happened."

"That would have been a surprise: the President's wife, just strolling along."

"Camp David is a better place for it. Sometimes I just have to get some exercise, though."

"I know. If I could be better about that, I'd take off the ten pounds I packed on last Christmas."

"Everyone comments on how thin I am. I did weigh more when I was younger. It's a very modern building, isn't it? Is this where the restaurant is that they say is so good? We could come for dinner after an evening at the Kennedy Center. Or maybe we couldn't now. What am I thinking."

"You can't give them any opportunity for a photo, because they don't miss an opportunity."

"That's for sure."

"Would you like me to turn around and drive past on the other side?"

"No. I've seen it."

"There are some businesses there. There's a barber. That sort of thing."

"Yes, I'd think so, with so many people needing services."

"So that was it. That's all you wanted to see?"

"More than I wanted to see. At least, for this reason. I should probably know more about the city. I'm sure there are many new architectural sights all the time."

"Look! Another one! Nobody's using his turn signal tonight."

"I used to love to drive, but driving here doesn't seem appealing."

"No, ma'am."

"So the guard caught them. That's when it all started."

"As I understand it. Yes."

Rashomon

He'll never get any credit for anything he says on the subject anyway. I wanted him to just state frankly that he didn't know, that no one knows, the full story of Watergate.

—Mrs. Nixon

Writers might sometimes think they are pretty competent discussing what they've researched, but generally, writers are the first to admit there might be more evidence or another perspective. Having the complete picture isn't necessarily the objective. Finding out as much as you can might be a goal—no different with fiction or nonfiction. But writers tend toward skepticism, extrapolating information not just from words, but from what's withheld, from body language, from facts that seem to exist in opposition to one another. What someone tells you will usually be her understanding of the truth. The next person tells you what he or she believes. A fact-checker might save you (every day there is less fact-checking, and more misinformation because of people's reliance on the Internet). It's difficult for fiction writers to reconceive dialogue because they've written it as they've heard it. You set a trap for yourself, of course, by seeming to control the external circumstances: you invent the room in which the characters have their exchange;

the snowstorm—because you didn't expect it, either—seems inevitable, but something else has determined the conversation. To some extent the writer is only recording.

In theory, you can move your characters out of the ski lodge and into the desert, but such revisions are so radical that I'd fear losing hold of the material and would rarely be tempted to make such radical shifts, though it is interesting that writers, themselves, move often or live in several places. (Hamptons envy: pictures from the party you weren't invited to; houses you'll never own.) Yearning is a necessary component to Americans' conception of themselves. Something always has to be the faraway green light at the end of the dock. New York–based publications could not fill their pages without this assumption. Capitalism would stagger and fall.

When Mrs. Nixon wanted her husband to say that the Watergate mess could not be understood, she was tapping into the American spirit, counting on the complexity and validity of alternating opinions, rather than offering a rationale for the bizarre break-in.

Why *couldn't* RN say, embarrassing as it might be, that he had no idea of the number of people involved in Watergate, and he had no way of questioning everyone? President Kennedy, used to poking fun at himself, could have passed it off as something that, yet again, he did not know enough about so that he had, of course, not acted promptly enough, then found some way to say this was because he was always outwitted by his charming wife, fluent in French and in the ways of the world. At least JFK knew how to appear abashed and to let the nation know that while they might be dazzled and charmed, he was (aw, shucks) just a hapless fellow: the guy who was always eclipsed by his wife and photogenic children. RN brought himself into everything and could admit no distance between his person and the presidency. He didn't believe it existed. Surprisingly, this Quaker thought he'd been born for the stature he finally attained, whereas Kennedy could afford to joke.

What if he *had* said that he hadn't kept a close enough watch, and that some people (he was certainly willing to sacrifice them) had acted badly, and that he apologized, and there would be no more of it? What if he had never made the fatal mistake of tape-recording his conversations in the White House, ostensibly for posterity, but more likely to be used as blackmail, and as a running ledger of who owed him? The White House had been bugged before, but RN was so incautious as to forget to deactivate a switch those times he would have benefited by something being off the record. Paranoia can be contagious. In the Nixon White House, everyone was listening in on everyone else. The panting on the extension phones must have been palpable, as Kissinger's people listened in on calls with Nixon, and his people's people listened in on yet others. Everything was highly monitored: only Alexander Butterfield might truly have been naïve enough to assume that all the listening in was in the service of the President's eventually writing his memoirs.

We have to wonder if Mrs. Nixon's phone was also tapped. It's difficult to believe it wasn't, just as a precaution, just for the hell of it. Though she was ignored as much as possible by Haldeman and Ehrlichman, nothing could be *lost* listening in on her calls. When she died, her tombstone bore the epitaph "Even when people can't speak your language, they can tell if you have love in your heart." Tapping her phone might have revealed just how much love.

The idea of love in one's heart is intriguing, though. It was what the activists and protesters believed, what the sixties believed: that if you were the right kind of person, language wouldn't define you—your *karma* would. You were either the right sort of person or the wrong sort. Mr. Nixon believed that what people said was one thing, but what he felt they believed was another. For example, whatever they said, they were suspect if they were Jews. If they'd been educated in an Ivy League school, ditto. Mr. Nixon did not come down firmly in favor of people being defined by their statements. After all, why would a man who never felt bound by the true value of words believe others? Of course, it would help if they had positive thoughts about Republicans and about his presidency, but that wouldn't be enough. Really, nothing was ever enough. Mrs. Nixon, however, believed that people should have good hearts and do good deeds. She was sincere, helpful, aware that she was a figurehead whose imprimatur could help various good causes, various good people. Nothing suggests that she thought herself inherently special, with a quality that would draw people to her. She was accustomed to reaching out, whereas her husband was accustomed to finding a way to draw people close. If Mrs. Nixon was Little Red Riding Hood (admittedly, a bit long of tooth), then Mr. Nixon was the wolf, disguised as Grandma, asking all the necessary questions, ready to pounce.

The authors of *The Final Days* present Mr. Nixon's mulling over of Watergate to an audience well within the fold: "Don't you think it's interesting, though, to run through this?" he asked. "Really, the goddamn record is not bad, is it?"

"Makes me feel very good," Ziegler answered.

"To the President, that was overstating it a bit. 'It's not comfortable for me, because I was sitting there like a dumb turkey.'" (See: Agnew, Spiro; also, the presidential pardon of the Thanksgiving turkey.)

"Ziegler had an answer. 'It's a *Rashomon* theory,' he offered.

"'Hm?' the President asked."

Here, the writer has to pause to appreciate what's about to follow. A likely interpretation of "Hm?" is that Richard Nixon had never heard of *Rashomon*. For one thing, it wasn't American, and foreign = other = not to be trusted. It was tied in to contemporary culture in a way he was not and had no intention of being. But Kurosawa's film had crept into our lexicon, as had the idea that there was no definitive story, but instead an amalgam of what people thought they saw and believed they'd heard, the way the frighteningly dismissive "whatever" has intruded into the language, giving carte blanche to signal boredom and indifference and to ask others to draw no conclusions at all.

"It's a *Rashomon* theory," Ziegler tried again. "Five men sit in a room, and what occurs in that room or what is said in that room means something different to each man, based upon his perceptions of the events that preceded it. And that is exactly what this is. Exactly what it [Watergate] is.

"The President grasped the point: Dean perceived that the President was involved in the cover-up based on his own, not Nixon's, special knowledge of what had gone before. It seemed to the President to be a pretty good theory. Perhaps it would hold up."

If Mrs. Nixon could have put a word in his vocabulary, it might have been *Rashomon*. It had a quality she understood: it's a complex situation, I don't know everything, no one knows everything. The movie had established itself as part of the culture: the part the President didn't trust, though he still might appropriate it in his own defense. For a man who thought he knew exactly what had happened, and exactly what right and wrong were, it was a timely concept—one that could excuse him, if he could use it to generate enough uncertainty and confusion. *Rashomon* hadn't already permeated his consciousness as a radical reappraisal of how to look at reality, but it was worth a try, the same way a superabsorbent dish towel might be used to mop up. *Rashomon*, one of those fancy concepts, probably out of the academy. Out of the movies, worse still. Not to dismiss movies altogether; he watched *Patton* over and over. (Now, there was a man who would have had nothing to do with *Rashomon*.) And true, he hired his staff from the academy. Kissinger came from Harvard, others from Yale, where probably unknown to Nixon, the pointy-heads—French pointy-heads!—were deconstructing the very idea of agreed-on truth. *Rashomon* with theory!

"Hm?" the President had said, having little idea of the way the concept had permeated the culture, defining it and reflecting it. He wasn't out at the movies, opening himself up to some foreign notion that could be insidious. There was already a lot of confusion, protest marches that were nothing but confusion, and unbelievable as it was, some people wanted to sink even deeper. He liked to play the game of engaging a new notion every time the mirrored ball flashed, only to decide against it as it twirled away—or maybe his deciding otherwise *made the ball* rotate. Then the next shining notion would send a spark of light into your eye and clarify something else, for a spotlit second. If you were paranoid, though, you'd think the mirrored ball was there to entrap you: something glitzy and pretty and mesmerizing, but surfaces could be only so informative. You would want to be the person who controlled the ball, not the person who danced beneath it.

Some dialogue, found on the Internet, from *Rashomon*:
Commoner: Well, men are only men. That's why they lie. They can't tell the truth, even to themselves.

Priest: That may be true. Because men are weak, they lie to deceive themselves.

Commoner: Not another sermon! I don't mind a lie if it's interesting.

Having recently seen *Rashomon* again, I find that this dialogue was not in the movie.

David Eisenhower Has Some Ideas
While Sitting by the Fire

M r. Nixon liked a fire in the fireplace, even during summer, when he would have a fire lit and turn on the air-conditioning. He wanted a fire at Camp David, the White House, San Clemente—and also at Julie Nixon and David Eisenhower's, those times the Nixons brought dinner from the White House kitchen. RN, himself, is said to have lit the fire. It may well be—but this is the man who, in frustration, tried to bite off a pill bottle's tamper-proof lid. But let's say that he lit it. They arrived at the Eisenhowers', RN lit the fire, and *they did not talk about Watergate* because no fire would be consoling and comfy if that—forgive the pun—hot topic was brought up. "My father first lit the fire," Julie Eisenhower writes. "While we sat in front of it, Mother would try to divert him by pointing out what was coming into bloom." Mrs. Nixon must have noticed flowers on the ride over, or when looking out the Eisenhowers' window. Since it was unlikely RN would refute her, or really even *hear* her, buds opening seemed like a safe subject. We all know what that's like: trying to find something diverting to talk about, so as not to upset someone who is already unhappy.

David Eisenhower's thoughts: My wife has decided the food needs reheating. It's also her excuse to get her mother into the kitchen so she can find out how things are going. But Mrs. Nixon's not responding the way Julie hoped; I can see the disappointment in Julie's eyes. When do I not, lately? My mother-in-law likes to linger by the fire, letting Julie reheat the food. If she isn't paying attention to what Julie wants, it usually means she's depressed. She feels comfortable here, that's good, obviously good for them to get out of the White House. They're so glad Julie and I still live nearby. I'd like to be in the kitchen, but I should stay with my in-laws—if nothing else, to fill what might otherwise be an awkward silence. There doesn't seem to be much easy communication between them. Wonder what the kitchen's sent over. I hope something good. Awful flap, that criticism of Heinz Bender—a great pastry chef, and some journalist got the recipe for Julie's wedding cake way in advance, baked it, and said it was terrible. Might be funny, if it didn't involve family. Not much seems funny these days, and also, the Coxes get to live in New York. Mrs. Nixon is saying something about flowers. Pay attention, David. Yes—given a garden plot, as a girl on the family farm; she'd grown flowers she loved to cut for bouquets. Daisies, in particular, because they lasted longest. I should remember that: a good future present. She's always seemed grateful for small pleasures. Her mother died when she was thirteen, her father not long after. Her brothers were good to her, but she doesn't seem to be in touch with them. Never mentions them. Mr. Nixon has just about finished that scotch. Mrs. Nixon, her ginger ale. The Secret Service and the chauffeur are waiting outside. What a job that must be, even if Julie thinks they overdo it from time to time. Well, in here it's warm and might be very convivial if Watergate had remained only the name of an apartment building. If only, if only. How much time are you going to waste thinking about *if only*, David? Also, imagine if there'd been no Vietnam. Julie and I couldn't even attend our college graduations because of the war protesters who showed up. The Nixons gave us a lovely dinner, but still. It would have been nice to have the option of going to graduation.

What should I say? Mr. Nixon is staring into his empty glass. Mrs. Nixon has stopped talking and seems to be mesmerized by the fire. Wasn't there a line in one of Brautigan's books, when someone says: "There is some of each of us in the fire"? Those titles! *The Pill Versus the Springhill Mine Disaster*. Not something the relatives would have read. Doesn't my father-in-law like the short stories of Maupassant, though? Amazed he wouldn't hate the guy because he's French. Bet he's not reading anything now unless it's a transcript of a tape. And all those messages from Haldeman and Ehrlichman, keepers of the gate. What was the name of that dog who guarded the gates of hell? Cerberus. Maybe they should rename King Timahoe Cerberus. Never comes when he's called, anyway—he's too busy eating the pillows.

Well, if the Nixons have a good, cheerful evening, that'll cheer up Julie, as well. Is there anything I'm not thinking of that might amuse them, get their attention?

Possibly: "Remember that Mimi kept buttons for Mr. Nixon's campaign by my grandfather's bedside in the hospital?"

Or: "Remember the time we were campaigning in New Hampshire and Julie and I weren't married yet, and they put me far away from her at the Holiday Inn, to make sure everything would be proper?" No: neither of the Nixons would smile about that, even now.

Better: "Mr. Nixon, if you'd been Alger Hiss—impossible, I know, but just for the sake of argument—do you think you would have asked to appear to refute Whittaker Chambers's accusations, or waited to be called? What I'm asking is whether there's an advantage to going on the offensive, and how might that vary from situation to situation." An interesting thought, but my mother-in-law wouldn't say another word the rest of the evening.

Best: "Another scotch, a little ice? Ginger ale? Let me see what Julie's up to."

Or possibly: "Mrs. Nixon, I know what resolve you have, what optimism and energy. Do you think if you'd had a different background, you might sometimes see things as being more open-ended? Because your life didn't exactly proceed by your being flexible, did it? It proceeded by doing what you had to do." *That'll be the day,* when I say that.

Go with: "Another scotch?"

The Death of Ivan Ilych

I van Ilych has already died when Tolstoy's story begins. We go back in time, and Ivan Ilych's movement toward death is narrated. We see that he suffers, as does his family. If you replace the idea of dying with Richard Nixon's misery about Watergate, you can almost make an exact substitution. Section VI of the story begins: "Ivan Ilych saw that he was dying, and he was in continual despair." Read: "Richard Nixon knew that he could not put Watergate behind him, and he was in continual despair." Tolstoy's story continues: "In the depth of his heart he knew he was dying, but not only was he not accustomed to the thought, he simply did not and could not grasp it." Substitute: "In the depth of his heart he knew he could not escape the results of his actions, but not only was he not accustomed to the thought, he simply did not and could not grasp it." This is why—as the tapes reveal—Richard Nixon goes around and around, conjecturing, entertaining a frightening variety of thoughts, keeping far-fetched and more cogent thoughts at bay, letting them come to the surface, acknowledging them only those times they seem to rise to the surface unexpectedly, like a drowned body. Tolstoy's story continues: "The syllogism he had learnt from Kiesewetter's Logic: 'Caius is a man, men are mortal, therefore Caius is mortal,' had always seemed to him correct as applied to Caius, but certainly not as applied to himself."

Correct, because we know our enemies are always trying to undercut us, tell lies, make every molehill into a mountain, because some have the time for that, while others have to lead the country. So let me ask you this: who's the President and who's some chump in a short story?

Mrs. Nixon Joins the Final Official Photograph

I said, "Oh, Ollie, we're always glad to see you, but I don't think we need any pictures now."

Dick refutes me. "Oh, come on, Ollie. Take a few shots." Tricia gets up and suggests we link arms. We form a line, and Ollie takes his place in front of us. If I looked over my shoulder, I know Dick would be smiling, and, really, I couldn't take that. Julie's been in tears, I have. What happens if you're a Rockette, and you have a cold? You go out there and take your position, that's what. A bit of medicine to bolster you would make sense. But medicine or not, out you go—out we go, indeed! When have we not rushed ahead, in spite of any protests made to Dick?—and you smile the family smile, and you try to get through the seconds, the minutes, until the helicopter takes off, and if anyone wants to photograph that, which they no doubt will, they'll see nothing but a machine, rising, flying, becoming smaller, disappearing. They'll read a lot into that. Right now, though, our hearts are breaking. They've already broken. If it has to be done, it has to be done. Ollie's been there for all of it, so of course he's here for the final photograph of the Nixons in the White House. Then we must speak to the staff, of course. They did their best to serve proficiently and politely, but forget manners, forget *politely,* they really cared, they have to know it didn't go unnoticed. We're not the only ones under examination here, yet we're the ones whose picture is being taken for posterity. Rose Mary hasn't been asked to sit at her desk for a final picture. Haldeman and Ehrlichman are long gone—otherwise, they'd be standing with us. Julie's at wit's end, Dolly feels that she's been drawn into a whirling tornado that might eventually put her down on safe territory, but right now she can't go anywhere.

The last picture needn't be posed, a perfect reminder of what we looked like in positions we never took, as if we were a chorus line, or paper dolls. David could be consoling Julie, Eddie could be doing the same, drawing Dolly's head into his chest, as if he were a barrier, and if she could not see beyond it, nothing would really be happening on the other side. The plane will transport us. California is there, earlier in time, *young.* California is young. And Dick: what is he thinking? That until the last, we have to be a united family, united for posterity, and also to act as the cross in front of the vampire, to ward off evil and repel anyone who wants to transgress against us, because we are the Nixons, like a lineup of suspects: *that's* the person who said the war had to continue; *he's* the one who explained to the nation what was best, and his wife, why isn't she looking into the camera, why isn't she trying harder? She became mute long ago, her younger daughter became the family spokesperson, the older one retreated, the husbands . . . they are the husbands. Yet I find myself yearning toward one of them, toward the possibility he represents. Maybe David or Eddie can change the way the picture will look, because if I step forward and see Dick in my peripheral vision, Dick will be smiling, seeming amused, in control . . . is there a chance Eddie could leap out of the picture, as he wants to, mess up the choreography, elicit a real expression from Dick? *Who* would have thought he'd bring in Ollie for this moment, as if it was just another day, as if Ollie would be here tomorrow for breakfast, and Dick could have him photograph Julie eating her muffin and David drinking his coffee? Dolly having her orange juice, Eddie having his boiled egg and toast? That would certainly surprise the nation: the Nixons, enjoying a last breakfast, still in the White House. From left to right—no political joke intended—Edward Cox (boiled egg; toast on the side); Mrs. Cox (orange juice only, thank you); David Eisenhower (English muffin; scrambled eggs; milk; coffee; tomato juice); Julie Nixon Eisenhower (coffee, as a prop); and me: I must be photographed with something, since a slender First Lady arouses suspicion, but who would be able to eat, at a time like this? Talk about my weight all you want, but answer me this: would you want to eat? And Dick: the full breakfast, starting with an English muffin, ending with a slice of melon and a lime wedge? Would he dare pick up the lime and let anyone see that his hand trembled? But tomorrow morning is a lifetime away, and what follows is farther away, still; La Casa Pacifica, California, the clock turned back—truly turned back; there are three more hours in which to accomplish things, three hours more in which to avoid errors that might damn you for all time. What to do with all that luxurious time? He gave me a clock once and I loved it, but I didn't know that every time it clicked, the future would become inevitable. We're lingering on the edge of time, doing what's expected, trying to make the best of things.

Just a minute before the photograph, Manolo came in with the dogs, who wanted what they always wanted: fun; food; attention. So many times, dogs have been brought in to be the recipients of our love, but there are certain moments in which dogs are extraneous, and their presence might as well be arrows, or whatever signifies our end, including the pop of a flashbulb that might as well be an assassin's bullet.

Picture made, what happens? We escape the picture frame and do *what*, exactly? Wait inside the airplane cabin. How much longer until we get to the West Coast? How much longer before we can attempt to resurrect our lives? After the last photograph, how much can anything done for future generations matter? You can only hope Dolly and Julie will have normal lives, and not have to pose anymore. Their husbands—let's be honest—are no help at all.

People keep their own distinct space in a photograph. If they don't, the photographer explains the necessity of standing this way or that, politely tucks a wisp of hair behind your ear, asks that you turn just a bit to the side. Then the photographer calls for another picture, just when everyone is self-conscious and anxious. A sincere smile is requested, one last time. Everyone matters in the lineup, ostensibly. Dick and I know otherwise.

"The Dead" in New Jersey, 1990

When the Nixons lived in New Jersey after his resignation, trick-or-treaters came to the door, and one Halloween someone stood there in a Nixon mask. Nixon had a face easily caricatured: the nose, in particular. The forehead, like something you'd rappel. The black, unctuously wavy hair. So there stood Nixon, facing a version of himself. This was a man who liked to try out possibilities verbally, posing hypothetical questions and answering himself seriously, playing solo devil's advocate and sometimes deciding in favor of the devil, sometimes deciding for his own better angels, but most often calling it a draw and leaving open options in which paranoia could fester. Here, behind the mask, was a mass-produced version of someone famous enough to be recognizable, but also manufactured with editorial embellishment: Nixon as seen in a fun-house mirror.

Imagine a holiday, an evening that held the possibility of providing a happy time, a yearly routine. That was Halloween at the Nixons'. A similar scenario also describes the early pages of James Joyce's masterpiece, "The Dead." But because it's fiction, we anticipate that the story will be exceptional, which often makes us more prescient than the characters involved. The characters are always inside the situation, so their perspective is different; we, on the other hand, are always outside. We read on a literal level, and we also hover more knowledgeably, canny about context. If we read the sentences "It was always a great affair, the Misses Morkan's annual dance. Everybody who knew them came to it, members of the family, old friends of the family, the members of Julia's choir, any of Kate's pupils that were grown up enough and even some of Mary Jane's pupils too. Never once had it fallen flat. For years and years it had gone off in splendid style as long as anyone could remember . . . ," we know instantly that we will be observing the evening that proves to be the exception.

Richard Nixon, however, opened his door as someone whose expectations were not sensitized by having understood how fiction operates. He also opened it as the President and the ex-President, as a person who had many expectations, though those expectations were always limited—tempered—by what could so often prove problematic. He opened the door as an Old Guy—even in the White House, he had been called the Old Man behind his back. He opened the door as someone affluent, being called on by his affluent neighbors. As a corny fellow, but one unabashed: he liked to play old songs on the piano; he liked musicals; he liked—he really liked—*Patton,* which he watched in the White House screening room over and over. He liked formality, too. Uniforms for the White House staff. For the women of the house, dresses and skirts, not pants. He'd always felt tugged in two directions, thinking it advantageous to fit in and be one of the common people, but having a taste for good French wine, so that he'd arranged to have his personal bottle wrapped in a white napkin when poured, while the unsuspecting guests drank inferior wine. What they didn't know couldn't hurt them.

He opened the door as someone not in the best health, shamed (but only if he admitted that), conflicted about celebrating—which meant including others—in his life of near solitude. "Well, Mr. President, it's a pleasure to meet you!" the man in the mask said. Monica Crowley writes: "A few other visitors in the crowd sported Reagan and Bush masks, leading Nixon to remark that he had seen more American presidents that day than he had in his entire life."

We can believe that he did make this remark, but it's difficult to believe that it's the way the story ended, or that what happened had the same emotional effect on RN as it does for us. For that, we'd have to go to fiction, where the writer could either imagine the more immediate thoughts of RN or extend the moment, so something beyond the obvious setup would be revealed. In fiction, the reader would be more informed by knowing the thoughts of the person who put on the Nixon mask, or by Mrs. Nixon's perceptions and reaction, than by RN's. How many seconds elapsed before RN spoke? What was he thinking in that time? Was he aware of Mrs. Nixon, and if so, what did he think her thoughts might be? What were the thoughts of the little boy who accompanied his masked father? This is exactly the unexpected moment that always gets things going in fiction, and a perfect detail, as well, in that it's both surprising and comprehensible: it's Halloween. This moment could only sustain itself briefly, though, before becoming the pivot for the story to change and move in an unexpected direction.

A fiction writer sees that this can't be a self-sufficient anecdotal moment, like the caption to a *New Yorker* cartoon. Told as a funny story, it can package the moment, cuing us to admire RN's quick repartee, but the fiction writer would have to rewrite the dialogue, for the verbal response is *too* clever, and therefore seems contrived (the writer's problem, not a psychological problem of the person adept enough to return the volley). We become suspicious, for we're asked to believe that the mask-wearing provocateur and a man who hated to be provoked patiently played their parts in sitcom time. This account all happens on the surface. Fiction lives in depth, layers coexisting with the spatial and temporal inevitability of an archaeological dig. Which is not to sound dutifully systematic, for fiction makes its escape when something original and informative, that seems slight, and therefore unorchestrated, blows past like a thistle, yet is later understood to have anchored itself with a taproot. Fiction may often try to mimic chronological time, but really it thrives on chronological liberty. As recounted, RN seeing the mask and RN making a clever comment happen in either real time or the conveniently speeded-up time of anecdote. The fiction writer would want to address slowed-down time.

Seconds, when you are recording them, are long. Like a poet or musician, the writer fingers them jealously, holding them in reserve, unlike someone who thinks of a story as a joke of sorts, culminating in a punch line, so that time can be marched through, because the goal—the end—is clearly in sight. The fiction writer would insist that we stumble. That we look at the many facets of what's happening. The idea is to make the reader not comfortable, but uncomfortable. When the reader is comfortable, he or she is essentially passive. To get the reader into the text, the reader has to be captivated or discombobulated. There are acting exercises in which the actor plays, for example, the roles of both the powerful and the powerless person. The actor doesn't want to fall into stereotypes, though, so she can't merely cringe when powerless, or continually bully as the powerful person. Of course, within each type we assume its opposite lies buried; we're familiar with the cowardly bully. Many truths have to be hinted at, so it doesn't seem the actor (or fiction writer) has merely come to a simplistic conclusion. How do you do that? It's revealed about you, as opposed to emanating from you, if you're a public figure. It will be recorded that you say "nucular" instead of "nuclear," and that you have habitual gestures you're unaware of, or that are interpreted differently than you intend. Public figures are easy, because they're on display. You have to catch them in a private moment to really know something. To know Mrs. Nixon in her early days on the farm, and then as a college student in California, as someone on the campaign trail, in the White House, behind the walls of La Casa Pacifica, in New York City, and in Saddle River, N.J., would of course reveal different Mrs. Nixons. We're all changed by time and context.

So how, exactly, would you begin to tell a story about the wife of an ex-President, on Halloween night, both contextualizing her and also ready to be ambushed by her (the character simply, unexpectedly, says something the writer didn't anticipate and doesn't know what to do with), or else you have to ambush her—put her in a context in which she can't immediately adapt, can't get away with being her usual self—and in that way expose something meaningful.

Let's say it's Halloween, and it's understood that she's a bit old-fashioned, a gentle creature who avoids the spotlight and who thinks the slightest thing (a few holiday decorations, or some special cookies) constitutes fun. Could you write the scene so that something in the mixing of the cookie batter prefigures what's to come, although neither you as the writer nor she as a character knows what that thing is? What is ever better than a knock on the door (unless, as Raymond Carver said, it was the telephone ringing; once, a person calling the wrong number inadvertently informed Carver that what the story he was working on really needed was a character named Nelson), let alone on a night when this knocking would be expected, so you can play with expectations? You, as the writer, might not see the Nixon mask until the moment it's there, in your story. If it is there, though, it won't go away any more than it will in real life. It means to be there. Perhaps writers, like Panthe-ists, believe that everything has a soul. So the mask is suddenly a given, and we have to watch for Mrs. Nixon's reaction. Does she see it first, and if so, can we see her expressing, or stifling, a reaction? Can RN be absent—not home, for whatever reason? Off bobbing for apples with Henry Kissinger? Should either of her daughters or their families be present? Probably she wouldn't be doing this if she were alone. What if it's one of the grandchildren, who becomes afraid of the masks before the Nixon mask pops up? Like any grandmother, she would be attuned to her grandchild, and it might have more impact if she saw it through the child's perspective.

The excited child opens the door, and Frankenstein and Casper the ghost and Marilyn Monroe and Grandpa are there, and the child, momentarily confused, calls out to Grandpa, and in that moment Mrs. Nixon suddenly understands that, to the child, Grandpa is always a man in a mask—a grown-up, a keeper of secrets. But the child realizes his mistake: it *isn't* Grandpa, but why isn't it? Where is he? For the first time, the child really feels his absence. So, without voicing the question, he turns toward his grandmother, only to see that she's locked eyes with the Grandpa man. Neither breaks the gaze. The child is not acknowledged. The child's world is going to end, right there! The one adult who's pres-ent is acting strangely, and everyone else has become quiet, which is a bad sign. Like a bull, intending to get the impostor to run, the child bends his/her head, imagining horns, rushes the masked per-son and hurls herself/himself right into danger, right into the tall man's thigh. There's a little boy standing beside him who starts to cry as if he, too, had been butted. The man stands still, though no longer looking at Mrs. Nixon. She's horrified at the child's having done this, she actually forgets that Julie/Tricia hasn't accompanied her to the door, she's turned away to get help. Her grandchild has vanished in the crowd; she should just march out there and grab him by the hand and make light of it, but she's done that too many times, she's tired of that role. She has no energy. Is her daughter on the phone, or sliding a cookie sheet out of the oven? Everyone expects something of her, the way people in bad dreams expect you to figure out some problem you can't solve, or you're expected to say something, but you don't remember what you're supposed to talk about. It's her whole life looking back at her, jumbled with expectations, it's mere coincidence that it's Halloween.

Mrs. Nixon Sits Attentively as Premier Chou Offers the First Toast

Who does that man love? Does he have a little dog, and does he touch his nose to the dog's cold wet black nose, or does he eat dogs, the way I heard in school when I was a girl? The kids said that the Chinese ate dogs. One thing's for sure: the world is full of misconceptions and vicious rumors. I suspect he doesn't have a dog or eat dog, either, that man standing and talking behind his six microphones, with his dark slashes of eyebrow. Who does that man love?

Catalog Copy

"Toasty comfort will be yours when you wear 'Patricia.' Made in Sweden, where the winters are long, 'Patricia' comes with the same plush, comfy lining used in Kris Kringle's sleigh. Give the gift of warmth. Special slippers for a special lady! 6–9 N, 5½–9 M. Specify Kremlin Red, Snowy White, or Sometimes Blue."

Cookies

"Shall I put this eggshell in the trash, or down the garbage disposal?"

"I don't want to be doing this. I'm glad to know that you've made these before and they've turned out, though."

"I've done my share of baking. I'll just drop this in the trash, and ask you for one more egg, if you don't mind."

(Opens refrigerator; opens carton, picks up one egg with thumb and finger, closes carton with other hand, turns, pushes refrigerator door closed with elbow.)

"Did it close tightly?"

"Yes."

"Okay. What we do next is add a third egg, because these seem a little small—let me just lean around you and throw this in the trash. . . . Then you lower the mixer blade by pushing your finger on this button on the top. Our butter is already easy to work with from the stick's having softened for a bit before we began. Preparing things in advance is always a time-saver. All right?"

"Do you mean 'All right' that we're doing this, or are you asking if the butter's soft?"

"I'm just commenting as we go along."

"I'd rather *not* be doing this."

"Hon, you'll come to learn there's no point in resisting what's expected. Sometimes it's best just to do what needs to be done. Don't think of it as an *issue*."

Mrs. Nixon's baking cookies with Hillary Clinton is an example of an *anachronism*.

General Eisenhower Tries Role-Playing

S ee how tenderly I pick up your hand? You're Kay Summersby, and I love you more than I hate war. If Dick knew, he'd find a way to use it against me. He'd make sure the press heard about it and then say that it wasn't how a great man should be judged. He's afraid of me, isn't he? Not that he wouldn't spill the beans about anyone, if it could help his cause. So here's the way it goes: I speak to you, and you're her. You can be sad or happy or whatever you want. And we're in the Jeep—pretend this isn't a sofa, it's a Jeep—and the United States of America is far behind us, and so is our past, and there never was a marriage to Mamie. It's just you and me, Kay, about to start driving down this rutted road. When I rub my thumb over your knuckles, you know that I love you, don't you? I can tell you things I'd never tell anyone—least of all, my boy Dick. But that comes later. We're just setting things up. You're her, and I'm Ike, the way I really *am* Ike. I'll say something, and you make any response you want. Those are the rules, so that's the way we do it. When it's your turn, who do you want me to be?

This is *fiction*. It also contains *anachronistic* elements, though role-playing undoubtedly took place before the concept was named.

Mrs. Nixon N + 7

T his is an Oulipian exercise. After every noun, substitute that word with the seventh noun below it in the dictionary (*New Merriam-Webster Dictionary*, 1989).

In the Checkers speech, Richard Nixon said: "A man down in Texas heard Pat on the radio mention the fact that our two youngsters would like to have a dog, and, believe it or not, the day before we left on this campaign trip we got a message from Union Station in Baltimore, saying they had a package for us. We went down to get it. You know what it was? It was a little cocker spaniel dog, in a crate that he had sent all the way from Texas, black and white, spotted, and our little girl Tricia, the six year old, named it Checkers."

"A man-at-arms down in Texas heard Pat on the radiogram mention the facts of life that our two yuan would like to have a doggerel, and, believe it or not, the day school before we left on this camphor trip we got a metacarpal from unison statuary in Baltimore, saying they had a packinghouse for us. We went down to get itch. You know what itch was? Itch was a little cockrack dogfish in a crayfish that he had sent all the way from Texas, black and white, spotted, and our little girth Tricia, the sizzle yellowjacket old, named it Checkoff."

Mrs. Nixon Explains

chilly tickle, the cold of ice cubes within ice cubes—my ankle, touched by his big toe.

This is an example of *irmus*.

Mrs. Nixon Has Thoughts
on the War's Escalation

"You and Henry ordering the 'Christmas Bombing' was pesky!"

This is an example of *litotes*.

Mrs. Nixon Indulges Her Feelings

E scape, escape, escape, I pray.

This is an example of *epizeuxis*.

Mrs. Nixon Uses Her Powers of Persuasion

I did tell Martha Mitchell she should get a bullhorn and have the driver take her around Washington to express her views, but you've always been chivalrous enough to overlook my stupid opinions, so surely you'll involve yourself in something more important than wasting your time admonishing a woman as hopelessly inept as me.

This is an example of *charientismus*.

Mrs. Nixon Reacts to RN:
The Memoirs of Richard Nixon

D ick writes amusingly, with a sense of what makes a good story. "During our trips to China and summits in the Soviet Union, Pat showed her mastery of the art of personal diplomacy. She shook hands with dancing bears at the circus, drew children to her in schools and hospitals, visited communes, factories, department stores, and danced a step with the Bolshoi Ballet school."

I could say the same about him, but his awkwardness is always part of any encounter, and his smile is too intense. People thought his smile was insincere because it was *such* a smile. He was more than a little inept. I always worried, myself, that the smile faded so quickly. It made him nervous to smile, so once he started, he either kept that smile plastered on his face or erased it immediately.

He mistrusted his body. He was self-conscious about leaning in too far, about looking at the camera or *not* looking. With his brothers dead, was he ever supposed to smile? He was caught between doing the natural thing—smiling at a bluebird singing from a tree, or at a plate of freshly baked cookies, or sitting in the stands and watching a circus bear, it was all the same: he was caught between smiling spontaneously and being inappropriate, because they were dead and he was alive, and his mother's eyes judged him like a camera lens, long after she was dead herself.

Possible Last Lines, with (Curtain)

"So you see, Dick, you can have a lot of things, but you can't have everything. Don't tell me you already know that. You don't know it, you just refuse to think about it."

"Do you see the way his heels are worn down at the sides? It's why he has that funny rocking walk, or maybe it was the rocking that wore down his shoes. Henry has no taste in shoes, does he?"

"Tell the truth, gals, how many times do we come to the last line and also get away as fast as if the curtain dropped? If our curtains drop, it's because we didn't hang them right!"

"The play *Abraham Lincoln*, written by John Drinkwater, opened a week and a half before Christmas 1919. The play was written in six scenes. In the last Lincoln is shot at Ford's Theatre. Secretary

Stanton famously remarks, 'Now he belongs to the ages.' Well, we might not get an instant epitaph, but when the curtain falls, it falls, and I suspect it often falls on silence. It's just my personal view. It's like death, itself: *curtain*."

(*Curtain.*)

 ONLINE EDITION

Volume 113 >> Issue 29 : Wednesday, June 23, 1993

No PDF Available

Patricia Nixon, Wife of Former President, Dies at 81

Los Angeles Times

Patricia Ryan Nixon, the poised, gracious "perfect political wife" through the roller-coaster rises and disgraceful fall of former President Nixon's turbulent career, died Tuesday at their home in Park Ridge, N.J. She was 81.

Mrs. Nixon, a heavy smoker although she never permitted herself to be seen smoking in public, died of lung cancer. She had suffered from lung disease for several years and was hospitalized last February for emphysema when the cancer was discovered.

Nixon and their daughters, Tricia Nixon Cox and Julie Nixon Eisenhower, were at her bedside when she died at 5:45 a.m. EDT, according to a statement issued by Nixon's New Jersey office.

For three decades Pat Nixon was always there, the loyal and sometimes obviously suffering wife standing stoically behind her husband as he pursued a career that took him to the unprecedented heights—and depths—of public life. The former first lady cried only twice in public— when her husband lost his 1960 bid for the presidency to John F.

Kennedy, and when he made his farewell speech on Aug. 9, 1974, after the Watergate scandal forced him to resign.

She once said her "only goal" was to "go down in history as the wife of a president."

Her reclusive years after leaving the White House have been described as "Garboesque," with her resorting to wigs and disguises to go shopping. She suffered a major stroke in 1976 after reading Bob Woodward and Carl Bernstein's "The Final Days" about her husband's Watergate decline and fall, and another stroke in 1983. She had been in frail health for years.

"She cherishes the privacy of her retirement years," daughter Julie wrote in her loving 1986 biography, "Pat Nixon: The Untold Story," which strove to establish her mother's accomplishments as the most widely traveled first lady in history with trips to 80 nations, her laudable addition of antiques to the White House, and her promotion of volunteerism.

One of Mrs. Nixon's last public appearances was in Yorba Linda, Calif., on July 19, 1990, for the dedication of the Richard Nixon Library and Birthplace, and at a dinner that night for 1,600 friends at Los Angeles' Century Plaza Hotel. The library, where her memorial services will be conducted Saturday, includes a Pat Nixon room and grounds planted with the red-black Pat Nixon Rose developed by a French company in 1972 when she was first lady.

"She is a true, unsung hero of the Nixon administration and our country owes her a debt of gratitude," former President Reagan said at the dedication. He echoed that appraisal in a statement Tuesday.

"She was a woman of great strength and generous spirit. In time of trial and turmoil, she shared that strength and spirit not just with her family, but with the nation," said California Gov. Pete Wilson, who will deliver one of her eulogies Saturday.

The Tech • 84 Massachusetts Avenue • Suite 483 • Cambridge, Mass. 02139-4300
p: 617.253.1541 • f: 617.258.8226 • Contact Us

http://www-tech.mit.edu/V113/N29/nixon.29w.html   8/21/2007

My Back Porch in Maine

The writer chooses someone, or a situation, from endless possibilities. The writer may not even know why. Finding out can be the point of writing the story. The brilliant Donald Barthelme wrote an essay called "Not-Knowing," in which he says, "If the writer is taken to be the work's way of getting itself written, a sort of lightning rod for an accumulation of atmospheric disturbances, a St. Sebastian absorbing in his tattered breast the arrows of the Zeitgeist, this changes not very much the traditional view of the artist. But it does license a very great deal of critical imperialism." Barthelme understands the process of writing so thoroughly, he might not realize how much such a notion might surprise people unfamiliar with the way writers write. Writers don't talk to nonwriters about being hit by lightning, being conduits, being vulnerable. Sometimes they do talk that way to each other, though. *The work's way of getting itself written.* I think that's an amazing concept that not only gives words (the work) a mind and a body but gives them the power to stalk a person (the writer). Stories do that. They don't let go. They infiltrate dreams, or sometimes even reach out, nicely, and ask the writer to dance. Barthelme's anthropomorphizing of stories brings to mind (this mind) parasites, whose existence depends on finding a host. But—in that analogy—certainly there are worse things than being the host, because it means that at least someone or something is looking for you. You're not what writers most dread: you're not alone.

Everybody likes our back porch. The mosquitoes would devour us if we didn't have the screen porch, but we do, and I hang out there. Every spring when we come back to the house I rehang the pig lights, and every fall we take them down—my husband suffers from pig lights guilt; I put them up, so he usually feels he has to help put them away. Over the winter they are hung from a hook on the back of the downstairs bathroom door, where they dangle in a sort of delicate pig lasso. If they were left outside, they'd be ruined. Hanging them every year passes for tradition and is a rite of spring, in my world. "Pig lights!" people say. Or they don't say anything: they rock in the rocking chairs and have dinner with us—herbs fresh from the garden—and the birds sing for quite a while and jump on the edge of the little fountain for a drink, and the chipmunks who live in what we call "Chippy Condo"—a mortarless stone wall filled with welcoming holes—dart in and out of the wall, into the ground cover, across the lawn, some zigzagging into our basement, where (alas) they liked to live before Chippy Condo got built. This year, one in particular liked to strut his stuff. He was slower than the others, and fatter. He was always on the run, but waddled and—if I may indulge myself—was a bit insouciant. We were amused by him, though he may well have been a her. I don't mind not knowing.

Italo Calvino, in one of the many reinventions of one story, in his book *If on a Winter's Night a Traveler,* writes: "Though I leave the house as little as possible, I have the impression that someone is disturbing my papers. More than once I have discovered that some pages were missing. . . . But often I no longer recognize my manuscripts, as if I had forgotten what I had written, or as if overnight I were so changed that I no longer recognized myself in the self of yesterday." I suppose that if you think of yourself as inextricable from your writing, it's disconcerting to see writing that is no longer familiar. Even stranger is the possibility that your identity is mutable and that you can't get back to your writing, exactly. It's general advice—Hemingway, among others, has urged this—to quit while you're on a roll, midsentence, so that you have something to reenter the moment you begin again. Good advice, but I never do it. I rarely get to end the day's writing with a strong finished line, either—any more than I can come up with a quick retort. I like the passage from Calvino because it's spooky in the way it suggests that after a short period of time, after sleep, you're forever different, in some way; if that might be true, it would explain why writers revise so much, each new self required to work hard, while taking the material farther away from the immediacy of its inception.

Along the same lines (no pun intended), this past summer I was on the porch, reading essays on poetry by Louise Glück, all of them astute, remarkable, succinctly written:

> *A case can be made that publication reinstates vulnerability, collapsing the distance between both poet and materials and poet and reader. This overlooks the artist's most stubborn dilemma, itself a corollary of distance: specifically, the impossibility of connecting the self one is in the present with the self that wrote. The gap is both absolute and immediate: toward a finished work, only the most tormented sense of relationship remains, not a sense of authorship at all. The work stands as a reprimand or reproach, a*

marker permanently fixing an unbearable distance, the distance between the remote artist self, miraculously fluent, accidentally, fleetingly perceptive, and the clumsy, lost self in the world. Critical assault of a finished work is painful in that it affirms present self-contempt. What it cannot do, either for good or ill, is wholly fuse, for the poet, the work and the self; the vulnerability of the poet to critical reception remains complicated by that fact. And the sting the poet may suffer differs from the risks of more immediate exposure: the ostensibly exposed self, the author, is, by the time of publication, out of range, out of existence, in fact.

That's it. You write by darting out of the spaces in the stone wall to show yourself and to go about your business, or just to have some fun, then return to hide in what have become, to you, the already intricate, private spaces, and whatever catacombs exist within the wall—whatever complex systems you use for protection and survival—nobody really knows. If you're a chipmunk, nobody much cares.

Finishing any writing project, I always feel myself simultaneously retreating. Though you have to stay alert, be open to possibility, continue until the last period, or whatever punctuation serves as your final, tiny ending, I still feel instinctively when I'm nearing the end of something. There's a second in which (because all writing is about altering time) things flicker into focus, though their illumination presages their diminishment, their going out of focus. The second you have it is the second it escapes you. So you let it go out into the world at the same time you retreat into the spaces between rocks. Writer as chipmunk.

Barthelme, in catalog notes to an exhibition of work by Sherrie Levine: "A picture on top of a picture. What happens in the space between the two."

Me, on Mrs. Nixon (I'm not using a question mark, either): We can't be conflated, but what happens in the space in between.

As with paper dolls, so with writing: pick your favorite and dress it, talk to it, *animate* it. That's how imagination works: you talk to it, it talks back. You're playing both parts until the moment the paper doll takes on a life of its own and says it wants to go live with someone more interesting, or that you have a big nose.

Mrs. Nixon didn't talk back to me—I'm not that far gone—but sometimes I'd write a sentence and feel it was my sentence, not hers, so I'd delete it and wait. All the while, I was reading books about *him*. It was difficult to lift her out of his context, but if I'd let her stay there, she would have hidden forever. She'd put on her scarf and go out only at night, *and not say a word to herself that I could overhear, because she wasn't crazy.* So I began to look at her in the background. Sometimes she came forward and sometimes she didn't. I left her where she was if she didn't give any inclination I might move her. I realize that I was acting on my own cues, but I began to experience the amazement James Merrill felt with his Ouija board, as he suspended disbelief and responded to spirits who gave him information. (If you haven't read Alison Lurie's book about David Jackson and James Merrill invoking the spirit world, do: *Familiar Spirits*.)

Mrs. Nixon didn't make it easy for a writer to write about her—nor was that any obligation. There *isn't* anything confessional written down (that I know of). We don't have the advantage of reading the stories of John Cheever and later—to our surprise—learning that we are suddenly able to read his diaries, so different from his fiction: such a different sensibility. Shocked readers held their breath until the next excerpt of his diaries was published in *The*

New Yorker. Of course Mrs. Nixon was interviewed by her daughter when Julie Nixon Eisenhower wrote her mother's biography, but the two were so simpatico that Julie Nixon Eisenhower was always highly aware of her mother's boundaries. How did Mrs. Nixon—rarely fierce, by all accounts—maintain them? I don't have the answer to that. Sometimes people engender enough respect that others back away. Sometimes they're lucky. There are many possibilities. Occasionally a photograph betrayed her true emotions, but she did not confirm or deny what anyone perceived. She didn't let us have a lot of information through words. I'm convinced she gave up on them.

I have no trouble understanding that. Writers may love words, but most also mistrust them. It's why so many writers like action: rafting; hunting; dancing; hiking into forests and countries where language, alone, doesn't define the experience. Words create an illusory reality. Being adept with language, writers often reel back from their desks wondering: does this just *sound* good, or do I mean what I've said? Sometimes the truth is, you don't know. Once it's there, the words arranged, alliterating and alluding, it seems shapely and eloquent, and its existence—its tidiness and length and depth—can seduce the writer as well as the reader. If it does, the writer will fail to write the real story.

Mrs. Nixon's prominence when I was a child and a teenager couldn't help registering on me, even if what I saw dismayed me and made me want to stay far away from that world. The haunting songs Mrs. Nixon and my parents' generation understood in terms of the war, I registered only as sad, filled with longing and promise. But those were still the sounds to which I fell asleep. I don't have love letters exchanged between my parents, but I do have a note to my mother that my father signed "Jimmie." He was so young, he hadn't yet changed the spelling to "Jimmy." I have a photograph taken in a picture booth of my parents, both nineteen, that proves they were in love, and that every real love is unique. Mrs. Nixon was my nonmother—my mother was youthful and eccentric, often one of the kids. As a voter, she was registered (I like the metaphor) "Independent."

Though there was a huge gap between my mother and Mrs. Nixon, I sensed that she was something my mother might have become, if not for fate. If you married a man and that man became something else, it could trap a woman. One possibility, when captured, has always been dignity: composure can (at least) land you, with a long pointed horn on your forehead, enclosed with a virgin inside a fence, around which flowers bloom. Not only I, as a young woman, but my mother before me, had escaped being Mrs. Nixon: domestic and modest; picture perfect; always smiling (such a wistful smile, though). A lot of people liked her, but something seemed wrong because she was married to *him*.

It seems obvious to me now that she puzzled herself. Someone who had what is euphemistically called "a hard life" moves on, having integrated life's difficulties. David Halberstam called her "heartbreaking." He said: "She ha[d] a childhood so harsh it is Dickensian." To overcome misfortune, Mrs. Nixon became a person who would try things, and who would persevere—quite possibly, it was a mode on which she overrelied. Nixon's immediate family vehemently did not want him to resign the presidency, even when there was incontrovertible evidence of his guilt.

There's all that—the mind keeps going back to that—though the birds seem happier than ever this year. Bright red cardinals (everybody knows those are the males) in among the pink roses, having a drink of water from the fountain, pecking beneath the bird feeder, fledglings learning to fly. It seems they all coexist: the butterfly moving off the flower for the hummingbird; the chipmunk disappearing as the rabbit hops out of the woods. Sure, you can sometimes hear the shrieks at night, find feathers on the grass. But as you rock, you can also have the feeling that you're pleased to be watching a life you're not orchestrating, and couldn't imagine meddling with. If you happen to be a writer, your thoughts might wander lazily: Did I write before? How exactly was that done? Because even if you stop watching, right that second, and begin writing, even if you write for a very long time and then get something down that pleases you and surprises you and all those other lucky things, you'll still disappear. You'll be a different you if your words are ever published, and there will be less and less possibility of ever connecting with them in the same way. You erase yourself every time you write.

The beach is ten minutes away, but I love to sit on my back porch.

Mrs. Nixon's Thoughts, Late-Night Walk, San Clemente

The Pacific is a grand ocean. It's oh so pretty to look at. He thinks so, too. We've taken many a walk here, but his leg's been so bad, he still can't walk. He's been asleep since just past dinner.

Oh, it will work out. It will be all right. The doctors have operated, and if only he follows their instructions, which I know he will, now that he has time to take care of himself, it will get better fast.

Even in such darkness, I can see the little whitecaps.

He used to take walks and think of me. He called me Miss Pat and sent me a note: "Miss Pat, I took *the* walk tonight and it was swell because you were there all the time. Why?—because a star fell right in front of me, the wind blowing thru the tops of the palms." Then all these years passed, and I got my code name, Starlight. We all got fictional names. I wonder if the bestowal made us just a little bit different. People in somebody's story that was being made up as it went along. Starlight reminds me of "Star light, star bright, first star I see tonight . . ." And there's one up there, tonight: one little star shining bright, people everywhere must be making a wish. Maybe Dolly sees it outside her window in New York.

Scarf double-knotted to keep the breeze from blowing my hair. What would be so bad if the wind blew it every which way? Out here on the beach with no one to see me, except my little friend the star. Off it comes, and I don't believe I hear any gasp from the universe. I'll put it in my pocket and fold it later when I'm inside, with nothing to do. If he'd come along, would he have remembered when my hair was strawberry blond? Silly Dick told me it was "titian-colored." He always did see things in his special way. When I worked at the department store, I'd try to show the clothes to their best advantage, daintily turning up a cuff, twirling a wide skirt. I'd put on a necklace so the blouse would get more attention. When a gentleman was buying a lady a blouse, he'd want to know if it should match her eyes and be so surprised if I said it should flatter her skin.

Did he get down on his knees with Henry to pray? Can what that book says be true? If I asked Henry, would he—even once in his life—be capable of just answering yes or no?

Quiet out here, quiet, quiet, quiet. That's what Aunt Neva said, when I told her I was marrying Dick. "What are you marrying him for? He's too quiet."

I got my first orchid corsage the day of our wedding. And Dick and I got orchids again, for the wives of the returning POWs. People decorate with them now, like they're roses. They don't seem mysterious the way they did, coming from faraway places. I've heard there's a grower in Malibu.

In the Peking Hotel the chef sculpted a praying mantis from a green pepper.

Now there was something unexpected. You wonder how such a creative idea like that comes to someone.

Such a lovely feeling, the scarf deep in my pocket. When men carry them, tucked in a breast pocket with just the edge showing, they never feel them, but this scarf of mine is my sweet little security blanket. I could lie on the beach and pretend the sand was my bed, and the scarf a cover, and the breeze an invisible ceiling fan.

"Star light, star bright, first star I see tonight, I wish I may, I wish I might, have the wish I wish tonight." They say no one knows who wrote that. It was written by "Anonymous." Lucky Anonymous, who never had to field any questions.

What to wish for . . . You won't stop winking till you hear what I want most, will you?

Chronology

3/16/1912: Thelma Catherine Ryan born Ely, Nevada, to a farmer and his wife; has half siblings and two brothers, Bill and Tom (both of whom she helps put through school)

1925–1929: Member of high school drama club; lead in junior year play, *The Romantic Age*. Also lead in senior year, *The Rise of Silas Lapham*

1926: Mother dies of Bright's disease and liver cancer

1930: Father dies of tuberculosis

1932: Attends Fullerton Junior College; lead in play *Broken Dishes*

1933: Attends one semester at Columbia University; tours the White House

1934–1937: Attends University of Southern California, graduates cum laude with B.S. in merchandising, teaching certificate for high school; many jobs (while in school), including salesperson at Bullock's Wilshire department store, waitress, librarian. Enters movie studio contest to "find a starlet" and is offered a job, but because it is for only one film, refuses

1937: Meets Richard Nixon when they both act in *The Dark Tower* as part of Whittier Community Players

1940: Marries RN (after much internal debate) in a rented room (the Presidential Suite) at Mission Inn, Riverside, California

1941–1945: RN an attorney in Washington, D.C., Mrs. Nixon a clerk for the Red Cross; RN a naval lieutenant, commissioned to Iowa, Mrs. Nixon works at a bank; RN to South Pacific, Mrs. Nixon in San Francisco as a price analyst for Office of Price Administration

1946: RN runs for Congress, Mrs. Nixon does research on opponent Jerry Voorhis and helps with campaign; daughter Tricia born

1948: Daughter Julie born

1950: RN defeats Helen Gahagan Douglas (who gives him the nickname "Tricky Dick") for Senate

1952: RN is chosen as Vice President of Dwight D. Eisenhower; RN gives Checkers speech after he is accused of taking campaign funds; Eisenhower is advised to drop him from the ticket; RN, in an unprecedented move, appeals to the nation on TV; Mrs. Nixon is silently present, as an example of their frugality and honesty, in what he calls her "respectable Republican cloth coat." The public buys it: RN stays on ticket

1953–1954: Eisenhower-Nixon elected; RN tells friend Murray Chotiner he will retire from politics after vice presidency ("I still resented being portrayed as a demagogue or a liar or as a sewer-dwelling denizen of a Herblock cartoon"); RN and Mrs. Nixon travel to Venezuela, where car is attacked by anti-American mob, daughters hear about this on the radio

1956: RN re-elected VP

1960: RN loses presidential election to John F. Kennedy by a slim margin

1961: Live in California; RN practices law and writes a book

1962: RN runs for governor of California and loses; RN publishes book *Six Crises,* writing about Alger Hiss, the allegations he had a private money fund, Eisenhower's heart attack, the trip to Venezuela, Khrushchev, and the campaign of 1960

1963: Moves to New York and practices law; Mrs. Nixon asks him to leave politics for good; RN is doing business in Dallas the day before John Kennedy is shot, hears the news on cab radio

1965: RN turns 52; reconsiders entering political life, breaking his word to Mrs. Nixon

1966: RN campaigns for Republican candidates

1967: RN travels extensively abroad; no mention in his memoirs about Mrs. Nixon being along

1968: RN runs for President; George Romney and Nelson Rockefeller withdraw; RN wins nomination and election

1969–1974: As wife of the vice president, and eventually as First Lady, Mrs. Nixon travels to eighty countries. Editing her husband's speeches et cetera. Mrs. Nixon acquires antiques and many paintings for the White House, holds "candlelight tours," has "Evenings [of performances] at the White House," feels there should be more public parks. She visits South Vietnam, the first First Lady to visit a combat zone (she favors amnesty for those who do not serve, at the same time she supports the servicemen)

1970: Mrs. Nixon goes to Peru in a humanitarian effort after the massive earthquake; shootings at Kent State (Mrs. Nixon is "appalled")

1972: Trip to China; Mrs. Nixon goes alone to Africa

1973: *Roe v. Wade;* Mrs. Nixon is pro-choice; she also endorses ERA, wants a woman appointed to the Supreme Court (and never tires of telling RN this). She does not get her way. She spends about five hours a day answering the majority of the mail she receives at the White House. Haldeman and Ehrlichman, her nemeses, and "two of the finest public servants" her husband has ever known, resign in the growing White House scandal about the Watergate break-in

1974: Return to Venezuela twenty years after initial tumultuous trip; Watergate scandal and eventual resignation of RN as President (Aug. 9, 1974), against Mrs. Nixon's wishes (her advice had been to destroy the tapes he kept of White House conversations, which proved incriminating); the couple depart for their home La Casa Pacifica, San Clemente, California, after a teary good-bye speech to White House staff, in which RN thanks many and forgets to mention Mrs. Nixon

1975: Mrs. Nixon gardens, has visits in California with her daughters, takes walks, is reclusive, worries about RN, who has physical problems (phlebitis that nearly kills him); RN is depressed

1976: Stroke

1980: Return from California to East Coast; live in East Side NYC town house

1981: Move to Saddle River, New Jersey

1984: Mrs. Nixon declines further Secret Service protection

1991: In a rare public appearance, Mrs. Nixon attends dedication of the Reagan Library with RN

1992: Many health problems, also diagnosed with lung cancer

1993: Dies at age 81 in Park Ridge, New Jersey; buried in Yorba Linda, California, Richard Nixon Birthplace and Museum

Notes

The Lady in the Green Dress

Hard questions on Vietnam: Joe McGinniss, *The Selling of the President 1968* (New York: Trident Press, 1969), p. 111.

Stories as Preemptive Strikes

In this chapter and throughout the book, I am indebted to Julie Nixon Eisenhower's *Pat Nixon: The Untold Story* (New York: Simon & Schuster, 1986). Subsequent references will be to *PN*.

RN talking to pictures: Bob Woodward and Carl Bernstein, *The Final Days* (New York: Simon & Schuster, 1976), p. 395.

Late-night phone calls by Nixon: Jonathan Schell, *The Time of Illusion* (New York: Alfred A. Knopf, 1975), p. 51.

"fragmentation": Ibid., p. 6.

Plan to get prostitutes to yacht: Ibid., pp. 205–206.

Mrs. Nixon after mother's funeral: *PN*, p. 27.

Raymond Carver, "Are These Actual Miles?" (formerly "What Is It?"), in *Will You Please Be Quiet, Please?* (New York: McGraw-Hill Paperback, 1987), pp. 210–211.

NOTES

The Faux Pas

"funny shows": McGinniss, *Selling of the President 1968,* epigraph.

Mrs. Nixon answered Wilkinson/Paul Keyes questions: Ibid., p. 157.

Mrs. Nixon, Without Lorgnette

Based on Anton Chekhov, "The Lady with the Little Dog," in *Stories,* tr. Richard Pevear and Larissa Volokhonsky (New York: Bantam, 2000), pp. 361–376.

"And it seemed": Ibid., p. 376.

"In his appearance": Ibid., p. 362.

"Why did she love him so?": Ibid., p. 375.

"felt compassion": Ibid., p. 375.

Chekhov's letter to his brother: "To A. P. Chekhov, Moscow, May 10, 1886," in *Letters of Anton Chekhov,* ed. Avrahm Yarmdinsky (New York: Viking Press, 1973), p. 37.

"How?": Chekhov, "The Lady with the Little Dog," p. 375.

Approximately Twenty Milk Shakes

Suggested by reading John C. Lungren and John C. Lungren Jr., *Healing Richard Nixon* (Lexington: University Press of Kentucky, 2003), p. 68.

Friendly, Faithful, Fair

Cold stadium: *PN,* p. 125.

Shoes in a bag: *PN,* p. 133.

Gift of bowl: *PN,* pp. 187–188.

Ernest Hemingway, "Cat in the Rain," in *The Short Stories of Ernest Hemingway* (New York: Charles Scribner's Sons, 1966), pp. 165–170.

"Time will say nothing": W. H. Auden, "If I Could Tell You," in *Selected Poetry of W. H. Auden* (New York: Vintage, 1970), p. 69.

"I love you": *PN,* p. 423.

Gatsby refutes: F. Scott Fitzgerald, *The Great Gatsby* (New York: Charles Scribner's Sons, 1925), p. 110.

"Yes, but": *PN,* p. 457.

"never get any credit": *PN,* p. 456.

Delmore Schwartz, "In Dreams Begin Responsibilities," in *In Dreams Begin Responsibilities* (New York: New Directions, 1978), p. 6.

The Quirky Moments of Mrs. Nixon's Life

Johnsons with dogs: *PN,* p. 250.

Queen at Balmoral: *PN,* p. 222.

Mrs. Nixon's Junior Year Play

A. A. Milne, *The Romantic Age* (1922; repr., New York: Samuel French).

Dialogue from *The Romantic Age:* act 2, p. 40.

Mrs. Nixon Plays Elaine Bumpsted

Martin Flavin, *Broken Dishes* (1930; repr., New York: Samuel French).

Review in the *Evening World:* Back cover, *Broken Dishes.*

RN's lists: *PN,* p. 152.

Mrs. Nixon Gives a Gift

"I have always wanted": *PN,* p. 82.

Guy de Maupassant, "The Necklace," in *The Best Short Stories, Guy de Maupassant* (Ware, Hertfordshire, England: Wordsworth Editions Limited, 1997), pp. 111–118.

Nixon's growing self-awareness: Lungren, *Healing Richard Nixon,* p. 38.

Caracas, Venezuela, 1958

Spit: *PN,* p. 174.

Commended by Eisenhower: Ibid., p. 175.

"At first the spit": Ibid., p. 174.

Mrs. Nixon's letters to her family: Ibid., p. 38.

"The girl turned": Ibid., p. 174.

Don Hughes: Ibid., p. 175.

"Muerte a Nixon": Ibid., p. 173.

Andrew Marvell: "To His Coy Mistress," in *A Collection of English Poems 1660–1800*, ed. Ronald S. Crane (New York: Harper & Row, 1932), p. 41.

The Writer's Sky

Keanu Reeves: "The Vulture Pages," *New York,* October 18, 2010, p. 115.

Frank Conroy, "Midair," in *Midair* (New York: Penguin Books, 1985), p. 7.

Katherine Anne Porter, "Virginia Woolf," in *The Collected Essays and Occasional Writings of Katherine Anne Porter* (Boston: Houghton Mifflin, 1970), p. 71.

F. Scott Fitzgerald, *The Crack-up* (1945; repr., New York: New Directions, 1962), p. 208.

The Letter

"Dearest Heart": PN, p. 68.

Mrs. Nixon Reads "The Young Nixon"

"The Young Nixon," *Life,* November 6, 1970, pp. 54–66.

Serving Mrs. Nixon First

Thomas Mallon, *Yours Ever: People and Their Letters* (New York: Pantheon, 2009), pp. 120–121.

Letters and Lies

"elaborate hidden machine": Schell, *Time of Illusion,* p. 70.

NOTES

F. Scott Fitzgerald letter: *Dear Scott/Dear Max,* ed. John Kuehl and Jackson Bryer (New York: Charles Scribner's Sons, 1971), p. 156.

Ann Beattie, "Desire," in *The Burning House* (New York: Vintage Books, 1979), p. 158.

My Anticipated Mail

Chandler P. Worley letter: *PN,* p. 80.

Merely Players

retakes: *PN,* p. 46.

drunk: Ibid.

RN as scriptwriter: Schell, *Time of Illusion,* p. 227.

Mrs. Nixon Lies, and Plays Hostess

News of Eisenhower's heart attack: Richard Nixon, *Six Crises* (New York: Simon & Schuster, 1962), p. 133.

"The Heart Attack": Ibid., p. 131.

Meeting the press: Ibid., p. 144.

"constitutional crises": Ibid., p. 181.

Prophetic Moments

Princess Diana: Geoffrey Levy and Richard Kay, "Yesterday Was Diana's 49th Birthday, and Her Sisters Wonder: What Would Her Life Be Like Now?" *Mail Online,* last modified July 2, 2010, www.dailymail.co.uk/femail/article-1291382/Yesterday-Dianas-49th-birthday-sisters-wonder-What-life-like-now.html.

Helene Drown: *PN,* p. 115.

I Didn't Meet Her

David Kirby, "Skinny-Dipping with Pat Nixon," in *Pushcart Prize XXXII,* ed. Bill Henderson (Wainscott, NY: Pushcart Press, 2008), pp. 259–261.

Flannery O'Connor, "Writing Short Stories," in *Mystery and Manners*, ed. Sally and Robert Fitzgerald (New York: Farrar, Straus and Giroux, 1969), pp. 96–97.

The Writer's Feet Beneath the Curtain

Edward Loomis, "A Kansas Girl," in *Vedettes* (Denver: Alan Swallow), p. 111–112.

George Garrett, "An Evening Performance," in *An Evening Performance* (New York: Doubleday, 1985), p. 12.

leaving the hospital after her stroke: Elizabeth Simpson Smith, *Five First Ladies* (New York: Walker Publishing Company, 1986), p. 93.

Joan Didion, "Why I Write," in *The Writer on Her Work*, ed. Janet Sternburg (New York: W.W. Norton, 1982), p. 20.

Gish Jen, "Duncan in China," in *Who's Irish?* (New York: Vintage Books, 1999), p. 87.

Mrs. Nixon meets Ms. Crowley: Crowley, *Nixon in Winter*, pp. 363–364.

Mamie Eisenhower Is Included in Tricia's Wedding Plans

Tricia's apron: From the archive of Howell Conant, administered by Bob Adelman, based on HC's color photo of apron.

"For Tricia and Ed It's No Secret," *Life*, January 22, 1971, pp. 19–23.

Mrs. Nixon Does Not Bend to Pressure

Suggested by *PN*, p. 317.

Mrs. Nixon Hears a Name She Doesn't Care For

Suggested by *PN*, p. 184.

The President, Co-owner, with Mrs. Nixon, of Irish Setter King Timahoe

"Holy Grail": Albert Goldman, *Elvis* (New York: McGraw-Hill, 1981), p. 460.

"big ones": Ibid., p. 466.

Mrs. Nixon Reads *The Glass Menagerie*

Tennessee Williams, *The Glass Menagerie* (1945; repr., New York: New Directions, 1999).

"gentleman caller": Ibid., p. 5.

"I don't daydream": Smith, *Five First Ladies*, p. 73.

Legend on screen, "Ha!": *Glass Menagerie*, p. 86.

"If you don't run": *PN*, p. 234.

"Où sont les neiges d'antan": *Glass Menagerie,* p. 27.

"You modern young people": Ibid., p. 110.

A Home Movie Is Made About Mrs. Nixon in China

Suggested by reading Richard Wilson, ed., *The President's Trip to China* (New York: Bantam, 1972), p. 22.

Cathedrals

"misleading phrases": Schell, *Time of Illusion,* p. 340.

Raymond Carver, "Cathedral," in *The Best American Short Stories of the Eighties,* ed. Shannon Ravenel (Boston: Houghton Mifflin, 1990), pp. 136–137.

Frescoes: Ibid., p. 137.

Host's religion: Ibid., p. 139

"It's really something": Ibid., p. 141.

RN's writing about Mrs. Nixon: *PN,* p. 414.

"It looks like": Stan Carter, "Hangchow," in *The President's Trip to China,* ed. Richard Wilson (New York: Bantam, 1972), p. 129.

What Did Mrs. Nixon Think of Mr. Nixon?

Alexander Woollcott and George S. Kaufman, *The Dark Tower* (New York: Samuel French, 1934).

Piano playing: *PN*, p. 25.

Engagement ring: *PN*, p. 68.

"shock": Flannery O'Connor, "Writing Short Stories," in *Mystery and Manners*, p. 100.

The Nixons as Paper Dolls

Tom Tierney, *Richard M. Nixon and His Family* (New York: Dover Publications, 1992).

"I'm gonna buy a paper doll": Johnny S. Black, "Paper Doll," 1915 (recorded by the Mills Brothers).

Rashomon

"He'll never get any credit": *PN*, p. 456.

Mulling over Watergate: Bob Woodward and Carl Bernstein, *The Final Days* (New York: Simon & Schuster, 1976), pp. 48–49.

Rashomon dialogue: information (apparently untrue) from Internet.

David Eisenhower Has Some Ideas

"My father first lit the fire": *PN*, p. 400.

Mimi: Ibid., p. 237.

Holiday Inn: Ibid., p. 236.

The Death of Ivan Ilych

Leo N. Tolstoy, "The Death of Ivan Ilych," in *Nine Modern Classics*, ed. Sylvan Barnet, Morton Berman, and William Burto (Boston: Little, Brown, 1988), p. 71.

"The Dead" in New Jersey, 1990

Halloween at the Nixons': Suggested by Monica Crowley, *Nixon in Winter* (New York: Random House, 1998), p. 365.

James Joyce, "The Dead," in *Dubliners* (1914; repr., New York: Signet Classics, 1991), p. 183.

"Well, Mister President": Crowley, *Nixon in Winter*, p. 365.

Raymond Carver, "Fires," in *Fires* (UK: Harvill, 1994), p. 29–30.

Mrs. Nixon Sits Attentively

Mrs. Nixon's thoughts suggested by the photograph, *President's Trip to China*, p. 22.

Mrs. Nixon Explains

Here, and in the following short examples, I consulted Lewis Turco, *The Book of Literary Terms* (Hanover, NH: University Press of New England, 1999), in the nonfiction category.

Mrs. Nixon Reacts to *RN: The Memoirs of Richard Nixon*

"During our trips": Richard Nixon, *RN: The Memoirs of Richard Nixon* (New York: Grosset & Dunlap, 1978), p. 538.

My Back Porch in Maine

Donald Barthelme, "Not-Knowing," in *Not-Knowing*, ed. Kim Herzinger (New York: Random House, 1997), p. 18.

Italo Calvino, *If on a Winter's Night a Traveler* (New York: Harcourt Brace, 1981), p. 186.

Louise Glück, "The Idea of Courage," in *Proofs and Theories* (Hopewell, NJ: Ecco Press, 1994), pp. 26–27.

Donald Barthelme: "On the Level of Desire," in *Not-Knowing*, p. 191.

David Halberstam's opinion: Lungren and Lungren, *Healing Richard Nixon*, p. 164.

Mrs. Nixon's Thoughts, Late-Night Walk, San Clemente

"Miss Pat": *PN*, p. 58.

"titian-colored" hair: *PN*, p. 55.

Aunt Neva: Ibid., p. 67.

"Star Light, Star Bright" really is by "Anonymous."

About the Author

Ann Beattie has been included in four O. Henry Award collections and in John Updike's *The Best American Short Stories of the Century*. In 2000, she received the PEN/Malamud Award for achievement in the short story form. In 2005, she received the Rea Award for the Short Story and in 2011 was given the Mary McCarthy Award from Bard College. She and her husband, Lincoln Perry, live in Key West, Florida, and Charlottesville, Virginia, where she is Edgar Allan Poe Professor of Literature and Creative Writing at the University of Virginia.